The Poor Doubting Christian Drawn to Christ

THOMAS HOOKER

BAKER BOOK HOUSE
Grand Rapids, Michigan 49506

Reprinted 1981 by
Baker Book House Company
ISBN: 0-8010-4246-1

PHOTOLITHOPRINTED BY CUSHING - MALLOY, INC.
ANN ARBOR, MICHIGAN, UNITED STATES OF AMERICA

CONTENTS

CHAP. I

INTRODUCTION

EVERY minister, especially if a pastor, meets with Christians who suffer spiritual trials, of various forms and degrees of intensity. His solicitude as a conscientious and affectionate watchman for souls, is awaked for such; while he yet feels uncertain on the precise counsels to be given, for their instruction and relief. A book therefore, which can be put into their hands, adapted to their necessities; which they can read repeatedly; by which they can examine their own hearts; over which they can pray; through the aid of which they can understand the causes of their sorrows, and find their way out of perplexity and darkness, into light and comfort, cannot fail to be esteemed of great worth. A book of such a character, it is believed, will be found in the present little volume. It will subserve the two-fold purpose of guarding Christians against the devices of their adversary; and preventing discomfort and mistakes relative to their spiritual state. The biographical sketch of the venerable author will apprize the reader how well qualified he was to deal with cases of spiritual perplexity.

Not only the private Christian but the minister will find this little work worthy of frequent perusal. As the physician avails himself of the books of experienced and skillful practitioners: so the Christian minister feels it a privilege to avail himself of the results of the studies, experience and observation of his fathers and brethren, who have been wise and successful in their treatment of the cases of afflicted and tender-spirited Christians.

That there is danger of "healing the hurt" of the professor of religion "slightly," cannot be doubted. Peace and comfort may be administered where they do not belong; or before the way is prepared. There are probably professors of religion who have occasion to stand in doubt of themselves. He in whom a worldly spirit predominates; whose example is inconsistent with his Christian covenant; who lives in an unsettled, uneasy and skeptical frame of mind, relative to great and fundamental doctrines of the gospel, or has adopted unscriptural views of divine truth; or who contends with those doctrines of the Scriptures which humble human pride, and show man dependant entirely on the sovereign grace of God; or who is endeavoring to make hope and profession the means of quiet, notwithstanding the disturbances and rebukes of a dissatisfied conscience;—the professor of religion in whom any of these things appear, has serious reason to be afraid of himself. The following pages do not appear to have been written for such. Fuller's Backslider; Mead's Almost Christian; Alleine's Alarm, and Baxter's Call to the Unconverted, should be recommended to their serious perusal. The faithful minister will make it one object of his instructions to disturb the peace of such, for they may be ruined by self-deception, except their peace be broken up and substituted by "a better hope."

This book therefore, should be read with a right understanding of its design, and of the precise class of cases to which its counsels are adapted. It is designed for "mourners in Zion:" for those children of God whose "souls are cast down and disquieted within them:" for those who "walk softly before the Lord;" who live in conflict with sin in themselves; who have been wounded with "the fiery darts of the wicked one;" and who would prize, inestimably, the peace and comfort to be obtained by going to Calvary, and in "sitting at the feet of Jesus."

It is probable that the present volume will fall into the hands of some who have prematurely entered the visible church. Views of religion have been taught in recent years, which have multiplied such cases to an alarming extent. Under the influence of erroneous instruction, many, it is feared, have made a profession of religion because they have resolved in a general way to live religiously, and have begun to do some of the outward things of religion; while, to use the language of David Brainard, they "do not see any manner of difference between those exercises which are spiritual and holy, and those which have self-love for their beginning, centre and end." The statement of such subjects of Christian experience as are contained in this book, may be met, by this class of persons, with the language of the skeptical Athenians to Paul, "thou bringest certain strange things to our ears." It is affectionately suggested for their consideration, that to have come into the visible church in ignorance of those spiritual affections which are produced in the renewed heart by the Holy Spirit, is to have taken a step attended with serious hazard. If he who professes religion, in ignorance or skepticism relative to the offices and work of Christ, in our redemption, does it to the endangering of his soul; equally does he peril his eternal interests, who comes to the altar of God, to declare himself a Christian, and to take a Christian's vows, who misunderstands, disesteems or calls in question the offices and work of the Holy Spirit in regeneration.

Should the perusal of the following pages induce in any who profess religion, a spirit of inquiry, a review of their religious course, self-examination, and the correction of mistaken views relative to the work of grace and its Author; and if any perplexed and trembling Christian shall be relieved, established, comforted, in being "drawn to Christ," it will not be in vain that the venerable author, in its re-publication, has broken the silence of more than a hundred years, to speak again, to the children of God, "the heirs of salvation."

The inquiry is respectfully suggested for the consideration of ministers of the gospel, whether the methods of instruction and counsel, exemplified in this book, may not be too rare, at the present day. Should not they to whom Christ has said, "feed my sheep, feed my lambs," cultivate that acquaintance with the members of their churches, and take that interest in their spiritual condition which will better prepare them to understand their religious trials, perplexities and conflicts; and more wisely and successfully to administer for their comfort and establishment in the hope which is in Christ Jesus. In such duties will be found some of the most interesting and profitable labours of the pastor. Good it is, thus to be laborers together with Christ, in " comforting those that mourn in Zion."

In the revision of this volume for the press, the editor has confined himself principally, to changes in the orthography, and the omission of numeral repetitions. The author appears to have translated his Scripture proofs for himself; which accounts for discrepancies from the received English text.

No apology is offered for leaving the author to speak in the style of his time. Antiquated though it be, in some instances, it has a simplicity and force of expression which ought not to be sacrificed to so unimportant an object as giving ancient thoughts a modern dress. Puritan thoughts are best expressed in the style of their Puritan authors. That is not good taste which would bring up from his grave a writer of another century, to express himself after the style of the present day: Moreover, changes made in an author's style, place at hazard the precise import of his writings; and thus shades of difference, or even something more important than shades, may be introduced; doing injustice to his true sentiments, and frustrating the original design of his work. There is nothing in the fact that a man has been gone to his grave a hundred years, or only as many days, to justify taking liberties with his book, which we should not dare to take were he living; and in which he may be made to speak unlike himself, either as to his style, or the character of his thoughts.

E. W. Hooker

Theol. Inst. of Connecticut;
East Windsor, Feb. 1845

BIOGRAPHICAL SKETCH

M̲R. Thomas Hooker was one of the most esteemed divines in England, Holland, and New-England, in his day; for great abilities, a piercing judgment, solid learning, extraordinary sanctity, deep acquaintance with the Scriptures and experimental divinity, and for awakening and successful preaching; and his name and writings were very dear to multitudes of the most serious Christians in those distant countries.

Dr. Cotton Mather tells us,—that "he was born at Marfield, in Leicestershire, in England, about the year 1586. His natural temper was cheerful and courteous; but accompanied with such a sensible grandeur of mind, as caused his friends to prognosticate that he was born to be considerable. His parents gave him a liberal education, and sent him to Cambridge; where he was chosen a proctor of the University, (whose office is to see good orders and exercises duly performed there,) where the influence he had in the reformation of some growing abuses, signalized him; and he became a fellow of Emanuel

College. The ability and fidelity wherewith he acquitted himself in his fellowship, was sensible to the whole University. And while he was in this employment, the more effectual grace of God gave him the experience of a true regeneration. It pleased the Spirit of God very powerfully to break into the soul of this person, with such a sense of his being exposed to the just wrath of heaven, as filled him with the most unusual degrees of horror and anguish; as broke not only his rest but his heart also, and caused him to cry out, while I suffer thy terrors, O Lord I am distracted. He long had a soul harrassed with such distresses. He afterwards gave this account of himself; that in the time of his agonies, he could reason himself to the rule, and conclude there was no way but submission to God, and lying at the foot of his mercy in Christ Jesus, and waiting humbly there, till he should please to persuade the soul of his favour : nevertheless, when he came to apply this rule to himself, in his own condition, his reasoning would fail him, he was able to do nothing. Having been a considerable while thus troubled with such impressions from the spirit of bondage, as were to fit him for the great services and employments which God intended him; at length he received the spirit of adoption, with well-grounded persuasions of his interest in the new covenant. It became his manner at his laying down for sleep in the evening, to single out some certain promise of God, which he would repeat and ponder, and keep his heart close to it, until he found that satisfaction of soul wherewith he could say, *I will lay me down in peace and sleep; for thou, O Lord, makest me dwell in assurance.* And he would afterwards counsel others to take the same course; telling them, that the promise was the boat, which was to carry a perishing sinner over unto the Lord Jesus Christ. Being well got through the storm of soul, which had helped him to a most experimental acquaintance with the truths of the gospel, and the way of employing and applying those truths; he was willing to serve the church of God in the ministry.

" Leaving the University, he now had no superiour, and scarce any equal, for the skill of treating a troubled soul. He publicly and frequently preached about London ; and in a little time grew famous for his ministerial abilities, but especially for his notable faculty at the wise and fit management of wounded spirits. Mr. Rogers, of Dedham,* so highly valued him for his multifarious abilities, that he used many endeavours to get him settled at Colchester. But Chelmsford, in Essex, a town of great concourse, hearing the fame of Mr. Hooker's powerful ministry, ad-

---

* The famous Mr. John Rogers, minister of the Parish Church of Dedham, in England.

dressed him to become their lecturer.   And about
the year 1626, he accepted their offer; becoming
not only their lecturer, but also on the Lord's
days an assistant to one Mr. Mitchel, the incum-
bent of the place; who being a godly person,
gladly encouraged Mr. Hooker, and lived with
him in a most comfortable amity.   Here his lec-
ture was exceedingly frequented and succeeded;
and the light of his ministry shone through the
whole county of Essex: and his hearers felt those
penetrating impressions of his ministry upon their
souls, which caused them to reverence him as a
teacher sent from God.   As his person was
adorned with learning, so his preaching was set
off with a liveliness extraordinary.   Yet the
vigour in his ministry being raised by a coal from
the altar, it would be a wrong to the good spirit
of God, if He should not be acknowledged the
author of it.   That spirit accordingly gave a
wonderful and unusual success to the ministry,
wherein he so remarkably breathed.   Hereby was
a great reformation wrought, not only in the
town, but in the adjacent country; from all parts
whereof they came to hear the wisdom of the
Lord Jesus Christ in the gospel, by this worthy
man dispensed.   And some of great quality
among the rest, would often resort from far to his
assembly.

   " The joy of the people in this light, was but

for a season. The conscientious non-conformity of Mr. Hooker, to some rites of the Church of England, then vigourously pressed, especially on such able and useful ministers as were most likely to be laid aside by their scrupling those rites, made it necessary for him to lay down his ministry at Chelmsford, when he had been about four years employed there, in it. Hereupon, at the request of several eminent persons, he kept a school at his own hired house, having our Mr. John Eliot* for his usher, at Little-Baddow, not far from Chelmsford : where he managed his charge with such discretion, such authority, and such efficacy, that he did very great service to the Church of God in the education of such as afterwards themselves proved not a little serviceable. In a manuscript written by our blessed Eliot, he gives a very great account of the little academy then maintained in the house of Mr. Hooker ; and among other things, he says, 'to this place I was called, through the infinite riches of God's mercy in Christ to my poor soul: for here the Lord said to my dead soul, live ; and through the grace of Christ, I do live, and I shall live for ever ! When I came to this blessed family, I then saw, and never before, the power of godliness in its lively vigour and efficacy.'

* This was afterwards the reverend and renowned Mr. Eliot, of Roxbury, in New England.

While he continued thus in the heart of Essex, and in the hearts of the people there; he signalized his usefulness in many other instances. The godly ministers round about the country would have recourse to him, to be directed and resolved in their difficult cases ; and it was by his means that those godly ministers held their monthly meetings, for fasting, prayer, and profitable conferences. He was indeed a general blessing to the church of God. And that which made the silencing Mr. Hooker more unaccountable, was, that seven and forty conformable ministers of the neighbouring towns, understanding the bishop of London pretended Mr. Hooker's ministry to be injurious or offensive to them, subscribed a petition to the bishop for his continuance in the ministry at Chelmsford. Yet all would not avail. The spiritual court sitting at Chelmsford about 1630, had not only silenced him, but also bound him in a bond of fifty pounds, to appear before the high commission. But his friends advised him to forfeit his bonds rather than throw himself any further into the hands of his enemies ; sent the sum into court ; and having by the earl of Warwick a private recess for a time, he fled from the pursuivants to take his passage for the low countries. At parting with some of his friends, one of them said, sir, what if the wind should not be fair when you come to the vessel ? Whereto he instantly replied, brother, let us leave that with Him who keeps the wind in the hollow of his hand. And it was observed, that though the wind was cross 'till he came aboard, yet it immediately then came about fair and fresh ; and he was no sooner under sail, but the officer arrived at the sea-side, happily too late to come at him.

" Arriving in Holland, he was invited to a settlement with Mr. Paget, at Amsterdam, but being secretly willing *Mr. Hooker should not accept the invitation, he went to Delft ; where he was most kindly received by Mr. Forbs, an aged and holy Scotch minister, under whose ministry many English merchants were then settled. Mr. Forbs manifested a strong desire to enjoy the fellowship of Mr. Hooker in the work of the gospel ; which he did about two years : in all which time they lived like brethren. At the end of two years, he had a call to Rotterdam ; which he the more readily accepted, because it renewed his acquaintance with his invaluable Dr. Ames, who had newly left his place, (viz. Professor of Divinity) in the Frisian University. With him Mr. Hooker spent the residue of his time in Holland, and assisted him in composing some of his discourses. For such was the regard which Dr. Ames had for him, that notwithstanding his vast ability and experience, yet when he came to the narrow of

* Mr. Paget, i. e.

any question about the instituted worship of God, he would still profess himself conquered by Mr. Hooker's reason; declaring that though he had been acquainted with many scholars of divers nations, yet he never met with Mr. Hooker's equal, either for preaching or for disputing.

"But having tarried in Holland long enough to see the state of religion in the churches there; he became satisfied it was neither eligible for him to tarry in that country, nor convenient for his friends to be invited thither after him. Wherefore, about this time, understanding that many of his friends in Essex were upon the wing for a wilderness in America, where they hoped for an opportunity to enjoy and practice the pure worship of Christ, in churches gathered according to his direction; he readily answered their invitation to accompany them in this undertaking. Returning to England, he was quickly scented by the pursuivants, (and remarkably preserved) but concealed himself more carefully 'till he went on board the ship at the Downs, which brought him and Mr. Cotton, and Mr. Stone to New-England, in 1633.* Mr. Hooker and Mr. Cotton were for

---

* She set sail about the middle of July, and arrived at Boston on September 3d, which glorious triumvirate as Dr. Cotton Mather calls them, coming together, inspired the people here with great and universal joy; as I remember the ancient people speaking in my youthful days.

their different genius, the Luther and Melancthon of New-England. At their arrival Mr. Cotton settled with the church of Boston; but Mr. Hooker with the church of Newtown,* having Mr. Stone for his assistant. Inexpressible was now the joy of Mr. Hooker to find himself surrounded with his friends, who were come over the year before to prepare for his reception. With open arms he embraced them, and uttered these words, now I live, if ye stand fast in the Lord. But such multitudes flocked over after them, that Newtown became too strait for them: and it was Mr. Hooker's advice, that they should not incur the danger of a Sitna or an Esek, where they might have a Rehoboth. Accordingly, in June, 1636, he, with about an hundred persons in the first company, removed an hundred miles to the westward, to settle on the banks of Connecticut river: who not being able to walk above ten miles a day through the woods, took up near a fortnight in their journey; having no pillows to take their nightly rest on, but such as their father Jacob found in the way to Padan-aram. Here (viz. at Hartford,) Mr. Hooker was the chief instrument of beginning another colony: viz. Connecticut Colony.

"He was a man of prayer, and would say, that prayer was a principal part of a minister's

* Since and now called Cambridge.

work; it was by this that he was to carry on the rest.   Accordingly he devoted one day in a month to private prayer with fasting before the Lord, beside the public fasts, which often occurred.   He would say, that such extraordinary favours as the life of religion, and the power of godliness, must be preserved by the frequent use of such extraordinary means as prayer with fasting : and if professors grow negligent of those means, iniquity will abound, and the love of many wax cold.   He did much abound in acts of charity.   He had a singular ability at giving answers to cases of conscience ; whereof happy was the experience of some thousands.   And for this work he usually set apart the second day of the week ; wherein he admitted all sorts of persons in their discourses with him to reap the benefit of the extraordinary experience which himself had found of Satan's devices.   Though he had a notable hand in discussing and adjusting controversial points, yet he would hardly ever handle polemical divinity in the pulpit ; but the spirit of his ministry lay in points of the most practical religion, and the grand concerns of a sinner's preparation for, implantation in, and salvation by Christ. That reverend and excellent man, Mr. Henry Whitfield, having spent many years in studying books, did at length take two or three years in studying men.   And in pursuance of this design, having acquainted himself with the most considerable divines in England, at last fell into the acquaintance of Mr. Hooker: concerning whom he gave this testimony, ' that he had not thought there had been such a man on earth ; a man in whom there shone so many excellencies, as were in this incomparable Hooker ; a man in whom learning and wisdom were so tempered with zeal, holiness and watchfulness.' When one that stood weeping by the bed-side, in the time of his last sickness, said to him, sir, you are going to receive the reward of all your labours : he raised up himself* and replied, brother, I am going to receive mercy. At last he closed his eyes with his own hands, and gently stroking his forehead, with a smile in his countenance gave a little groan, and expired, on July 7th, 1647. In which last hours the glorious peace of soul which he had enjoyed without any interruption for near thirty years together, so gloriously accompanied him, that a worthy spectator then writing to Mr. Cotton, a relation thereof, made this reflection ; ' truly sir, the sight of his death will make me have more pleasant thoughts of death than ever I yet had in my life !' Thus lived and died one of the first three. He of whom his pupil Mr. Ash† gives this testi-

* So Dr. C. Mather expressed it to me.

† I suppose the Rev and famous Mr. Simeon Ash, of London : and by this he means old England; and by the other, New.

mony ; ' for his great abilities and glorious services, both in this and the other England, he de-
serves a place in the first rank of them whose
lives are of late recorded.' "

These are so many passages recited from his
life, written by Dr. Cotton Mather ; who also
calls him, the light of the western churches and
pillar of Connecticut Colony ; and declares, that
yet he has underdone in this part of his compo-
sure : and Dr. Increase Mather, writing of Mr.
Hooker, says ; so good and so great a man ; than
whom Connecticut never did, and perhaps never
will see a greater person ; and that Dr. Ames
used to say, he never knew his equal.

As to the following treatise,—it evidently
breathes his most pious spirit, and shows his inti-
mate acquaintance with heart-religion. It is delivered in the plainest and most familiar language,
void of all ornament, as if he were speaking pri-
vately to some distressed soul ; which was his
usual manner in his practical discourses, as being
more adapted to reach the heart, than please the
imagination. And this admirable condescension
in a man of such vast abilities, is a clear discove-
ry of the real greatness of his holy soul.

It seems to be but part of others on the same
text, delivered to a popular auditory, taken in
short hand by one of his hearers in England, and
published there, after his coming over hither,

without his knowledge, as many if not most of his practical Discourses were ; as also with divers mistakes committed by transcribers and printers, which I have endeavoured to correct. And for the reader's clearer understanding the particular purport of the several parts, I have presumed to divide the treatise into chapters, and set the heads in the former margin for their titles, in this, which I guess to be about the seventh edition.

I would recommend it to those desirous of having the impediments which hinder them from applying by faith to Christ, removed ; and by divine help, would learn the happy way of going first to the promises of Christ, and then therewith to Christ himself ; and in this way daily living on him and deriving from him all their strength and blessedness.

And may the Divine Spirit attend it to the soul of every one that reads it ; and by promoting the life of faith, and other parts of sanctification, increase their present comfort, and the glory of the Divine Redeemer, as well as their mutual joy with him and this blessed instrument of his, when they shall meet together in the growing world above : Amen.

THOMAS PRINCE

Boston, April 1, 1743

SUPPLEMENT TO THE BIOGRAPHICAL SKETCH

It may be interesting to the reader to know the
esteem in which the venerable author of this little
volume was held by such men as the Rev. THOMAS
SHEPARD, first minister of Cambridge, Massachu-
setts, and JOHN COTTON, who came to this country
about the same time.

Mr. Shepard, in giving the reasons for coming
to New England, assigns as his third,

"I saw the Lord departed from England when
MR. HOOKER and MR. COTTON were gone; and I
saw the hearts of most of the godly set and bent
that way, and I did think I should feele many
miseries if I stayed behind.*

Mr. John Cotton, thus coupled with Hooker, it
appears, wrote a "Funeral Elegy" upon his esteemed and revered associate; an extract from
which, as the testimony of such a good man to
his excellence of character, may properly be given
here.

"Paul in the pulpit, Hooker could not reach,
  Yet did he Christ in spirit so lively preach,
That living hearers thought he did inherit,
  A double portion of Paul's lively spirit.

* Autobiography of Thomas Shepard, p. 43.

" Prudent in rule, in argument quick, full,
   Fervent in prayer, in preaching powerful,
That well did learned AMES record bear,
   The like to him he never went to hear.

" Twas of *Geneva's worthies* said with wonder,
   (Those wonders three,) Farell was wont to thunder,
Viret, like rain, on tender grass to shower ;
   But *Calvin* lively oracles to pour.

" All these in HOOKER's spirit did remain,
   A son of thunder, and a shower of rain ;
A pourer forth of lively oracles,
   In saving souls the sum of miracles.

" Now blessed HOOKER thou art set on high,
   Above the thankless world and cloudy skie;
Do thou of all thy labours reap the crown,
   Whilst we here reap the seed which thou hast sown "*

   * Autobiography of Thomas Shepard, p. 107, 108.

THE POOR DOUBTING CHRISTIAN

DRAWN TO CHRIST

Every man therefore that hath heard, and hath learned of
the Father, cometh unto me.   JOHN vi. 45.

CHAPTER I

Impediments which hinder souls from coming to
Christ, removed

THERE are divers impediments which hinder
poor Christians from coming to Christ ; all
which I desire to reduce to these following heads,

I. First, such hinderances as really keep men
from coming to take hold of Christ at all ; which
are briefly these.

1. Blind, careless, or presumptuous security ;
whereby men content themselves with their present condition, presuming all is well with them,
when there is no such matter.

2. Being convinced of this, they bethink how
to save themselves by their own strength ; and
thereupon set upon a reformation of life, thinking
to make God amends by reforming some sins

which they hear themselves reproved of by the ministers.

3. The sinner being convinced of his utter inability to please God in himself, at length gets up a stair higher, and sees all his performances, and prayers, and duties to be of no power in themselves, but that he must leave all, and cleave only unto Christ by faith ; and this he thinks he can do well enough, and so thrusts himself upon Christ, thinking all the work is then done, and no more to be looked after.

4. If he sees this fails him too, then he goes yet further, and confesseth he cannot come to Christ, except Christ give him his hand, and help him up ; therefore now he will attend on the ordinances, and labour and bestir himself hard in the use of all good means, conceiving thereby to hammer out at last a faith of his own to make him happy. And here he rests, hanging as it were upon the outside of the ark so long, till at last the waves and winds growing fierce and violent, he is beaten off, and so sinks forever.

II. Besides these, there are other kinds of hinderances which do not indeed deprive a man of title and interest to eternal happiness, but make the way tedious and uncomfortable, so that he cannot come to Christ so readily as he desires and longs to do : the ground whereof is this ; when men, out of carnal reason, contrive another

way to come to Christ than ever he ordained or
revealed ; when we set up our standards by God's
standard, or our threshold by his, Ezek. 43, 8,
and out of our own imagination, make another
state of believing than ever Christ required or ordained. No marvel that we come short of him :
for thus we put rubs, and make bars in our way :
we manacle our hands, and fetter our feet, and
then say that we cannot take, nor go. Thus it
is with you poor Christians, and the fault is your
own. But among many there be
three hinderances which are chiefly *Three main*
to be observed, by which many gra- *hinderances*
cious hearts are marvelously hinder- *which keep*
ed from coming to, and receiving *men from*
that comfort from Christ which they *Christ.*
might, and he is willing to impart
unto them.

1. The distressed soul, being, haply, truly
humbled, takes notice of the beauty of holiness,
and the image of God stamped on the hearts of his
children, and of all those precious promises which
God hath made to all that are his ; now the soul
seeing these, begins thus to reason with itself,
and saith, " surely if I were so holy and so gracious, then I might have hope to receive the pardon of my sins : or were my heart so enlarged to
duties, and could my heart be so carried with
power against my corruptions, to master them,

then there were some hope.   But when I have
no power against sin, nor any heart to seek so
importunately for a Christ, how dare I think that
any mercy belongs to me, having so many wants?"
Thus they dare not come to the promise ; and
they will not venture upon it, because they have
not that enlargement to duties, and that power
against corruption which sometimes the saints of
God have.

But we must know, this doth not hinder ; and
that we make that a hinderance, which, in truth,
is none.   For (observe it) we must not think to
bring our enlargements and hope to the promise,
but go to the promise for them.   Hope must be
stirred, and desire quickened, and love and joy
kindled by the promise.   But who made this condition of the covenant, that a man must have so
much of enlargement, before he can come to the
promise ?   Our Saviour being our husband, requires no portion with us, nor ever looked after
any.   All that he looks for is mere poverty and
emptiness.   If thou hast nothing, yet he will have
thee with thy nothing ; provided that thou wilt
have him.   Therefore it is thus written, *the rich
he sends away empty*, but the poor he satisfies,
and the thirsty he refreshes with good ; and so,
as that there is nothing required on our side but
to receive him as a husband.   For, *buy without
money*, is the text.   You must not come and think

to buy a husband. The Lord looks for no power
or sufficiency from you, of yourselves; nor of
yourselves any power against corruption, or enlargement to duties. If you will be content that
Christ shall take all from you, and dispose of you
and all; then take a Saviour, and then you have
him.

But the poor soul saith, if I go thus hood-
winked, how shall I know that I do not presume,
and how shall I know that I have a true title to
the promise?

I answer: there is no better argument in the
world to prove that thou hast an interest in Christ,
than this, which is thy taking of the Lord Christ
as a Saviour wholly, and as an husband only,
John 1, 12. *As many as received him, to them
he gave power to become the sons of God, even to
them that believe on his name.* He doth not say,
to as many as had such enlargement to duties,
and such power against corruption; but if thou
wilt take Christ upon those terms on which he
offers himself. There is no better argument under heaven than that, to prove that thou hast a
title to the promise. Indeed there is a desperate
despair that often seizeth upon the hearts of distressed sinners.

Therefore in the second place, as the sinner
looks upon the excellency of Christ and of grace,
and upon his own insufficiency withal, which

makes him that he will not venture upon the promise ; so he looks too altogether upon his own sinfulness and worthlessness, and therefore dare not venture upon it. He views the number of his sins so many and vile, and the continuance of them so long, and durable ; and he seeth the floods of abominations coming in so amain upon his soul, and Satan to boot, (who helps him forward in all this,) therefore he dares not make out unto Christ. But this is the policy of the devil, who (if he can) will make a man to see sin through his own spectacles, or not to see it at all ; and then to say, there is mercy enough in a Saviour, and therefore I may live as I list. But when the sinner will needs see his sin, then he will let him see nothing but sin ; and this, to the end that he may despair for ever.

Now here the poor sinner is at a stand, and can go no further. For tell him of the mercy of God, and of the plenteous redemption in Christ, and of the riches of the freeness of God's grace : " what (saith he) should I think there is any mercy for me, and that I have any interest in Christ ? That were strange." And thus the soul is always poring, and always too much fastened and settled upon his corruptions ; ever stirring the sore, without ever going to the physician. Where note, that a man is as well kept from looking to Christ by despair, as by presumption. Before he sees his sin, he thinks his condition is good, and that he hath a sufficiency of his own, and needs not go to Christ, and when he sees his sin, then he beholds so much vileness in himself, and in it, that he dares not go to Christ, lest when he comes before him, he sends him down to that ever-burning lake of fire and brimstone. Herein the devil is very subtile : but this doth not hinder our title to Christ; neither ought it to discourage us from laying hold on salvation. For,

1. Observe it, for whom did Christ come into the world, and for whom did he die when he was come ? Was it for the righteous ? Such needed him not : it was for the poor sinner that judgeth himself, that condemns himself, and that finds he cannot save himself. Paul saith, 2 Tim. 1, 15. *Christ Jesus came into the world to save sinners, of whom I am the chief.* And the prophet Zech. 13, 1. *There is a fountain opened for sin and for uncleanness ;* that is, for all sorts of sins, and kinds of sinners; be their iniquities ever so great, and ever so vile, there is a fountain set open for them ; come who will. There was never any saved that was not a rebel first ; nor any received to mercy, that first opposed not the mercies of God, and his grace in Christ. The fiery serpents did sting the people in the wilderness ; first then they were stung, and being stung, there was a brazen serpent to heal them. But,

2. Observe the folly of this plea: what Scripture ever said, that the greatness of man's sin could hinder the greatness of God's mercy? No Scripture saith so; we see David prayeth to the contrary, Psalm 25, 11, *Have mercy upon me, O Lord, and pardon my sins, for they are great.* Nay, God himself doth quite the contrary, Isaiah 43, 24, 25, *Thou hast made me serve with thy sins, and wearied me with thine iniquities; yet I am he that blotteth out thy transgressions for my name's sake.* When the Jews did tire God with their distempered manners, and burthened him with their sinful courses; then the Lord, for his own names sake, would not so much as remember their iniquities against them.

3. Again observe, that sins, though they be never so heinous of themselves, yet if the soul can see them, and the heart be burdened with them, they are so far from hindering the work of faith, and from making thee incapable of mercy, that they fit thee the rather to go to Christ. The truth is, (which I pray you to notice,) it is not properly our unworthiness, but our pride and haughtiness that hinder us from coming to Christ; for we would have something from ourselves, and not all from him. But to the distressed soul, that sees the vileness of his sins; I say, suppose thy sins were fewer; yet upon such a supposition, thou wouldest not go to Christ, as persuaded of

the freeness of his grace, but because thy sins are
not many, and upon conceit that thou hast a wor-
thiness in thyself, and wouldest bring something
to Christ, and not receive all from him ; therefore thou keepest back. And is it not plain then
that it is thy pride and thy self-conceitedness that
hinders thee ? Thou thinkest thou must have
thus much grace and holiness ; and Christ must
not justify the ungodly, but the godly man. But
I tell thee, that, upon such terms, he will never
justify thee, or any man while the world stands.

But the soul replies again ; my sins are worse
than so, not only because they are many, but because of the mercy and salvation that I have rejected, and which have been offered me from day
to day.

But, I answer : this cannot hurt thee, provided that thou canst see those evils of thine ; for
then, though thou hast cast away the kindness of
the Lord, yet the Lord will not cast thee away, if
thou wilt come and seek him earnestly again and
again. Isaiah 57, 17, 18. *For the iniquity of his
covetousness I was wroth* (saith God) *and I smote
him; I hid myself, and he went on froward y in the
way of his own heart*. If this could have hindered,
Judah should never have received mercy : but
the text saith, *I have seen his ways and will heal
him*. Jer. 3, 1. *Thou hast played the harlot
with many lovers, yet return again unto me, saith*

the Lord. So then, there is no time past, if a
man has but a heart to return. There is no lim-
itation of the riches of God's free grace, except
the sin against the Holy Ghost, therefore saith
Christ, Rev. 3, 20. *I stand at the door and
knock.* Though he cry 'till he be hoarse, and
stand 'till he be weary, yet he stands still: if any
adulterous or deceitful wretch open, the Lord will
come in, and bring store of comfort to him, and
sup with him.

Object. "Oh, all that is true, (saith the poor
soul,) had I but a heart to mourn for my baseness.
See my sins I do, but this is my misery, I cannot
be burdened with them ; I have a heart that cannot break and mourn for dishonouring God, and
offending him so many ways."

Answ. This hurts not either; provided that
thy heart be weary of itself, because it cannot be
weary of sin. Micah 7, 18. *The Lord sheweth
mercy, because he will shew mercy :* it is not because thou canst please him, but because mercy
pleaseth him. When did the Lord shew mercy
to Paul? I say, when, but even when Paul did
express most malice against him? Acts 16.
Saul, Saul, why persecutest thou me ? He per-
secutes Christ, and yet Christ pities him, and
shews him mercy. And so the churlish jailor,
when he was most opposite against the means of
grace, the Lord even then shewed most compas-

sion upon him. He that before resisted the
means of grace, was now brought home by those
means that before he resisted.

Object. "But wo to me, saith the poor soul,
you are now come to the quick ; this very word is
like a millstone about my neck, and I in the sea,
ready to be sunk for ever. This is the depth of
that baseness that lies on me, even this, that all
the means can do no better upon me. Why, what
though Paul and the jailor were bad enough, so
bad as you say ? Yet they were made better by
the means : but this is my hopeless condition, that
the means of grace prevail nothing on me. Oh,
is there such an heart in hell as I have ? For
how bad must it needs be, when all the means in
the world can do it no more good ! And now, methinks I feel my heart more hard and inexorable
under all God's ordinances, than when at first I
believed. My condition therefore is most certainly hopeless, seeing the means that should
soften me, do but harden me, and make me
worse."

Answ. This is the last plea whereby the devil
keeps in, and possesseth the heart of a poor heart-
less* sinner. But let me answer thee, and I say :
this hurts not either : for here at least thou mayst
have hope of mercy ! And here observe three
things by way of answer, and know that,

* Disheartened. Ed.

1. The word and means of grace do work good, if they make thee more sensible of thy hardness and deadness. Though haply they work not that good, and after that manner that thou desirest; yet if they make thee to see thy baseness, thy hardness of heart, and dulness of spirit, in regard of that body of death which hangs upon thee, then the word and they work in the best manner; because it is after God's manner, howsoever not after thine. That physic works most kindly, that makes the party sick before it works: so it is with the word. Before, thou hadst a proud heart, and didst therefore lift up thyself in thine own abilities, and didst trust in thine own strength, and thou thoughtest that thy care, and the improvement of the means, would work wonders. But now the word works sweetly, when it makes thee apprehensive, that a wounded soul is the gift of God, not of man, nor of the means; when it makes thee look up to God for it, and to prize it when thou hast it; and to wait upon God with thy daily prayers, still to continue it so. To feel deadness, is life; and to feel hardness is softness. Only remember this one caution; except there be some lust or distemper that thy heart hankers after, (for then the word will harden thee, because thou hardenest thyself) that one I say excepted, thou art in a good way.

2. Mark this, I beseech you thou art the

cause why thy heart is not softened, and why the word works not upon thy soul. The distemper of thine own heart, hinders the working of the word, and dispensation of God's providence, and the tenour of the covenant of grace. Thou thinkest to limit the holy one of Israel; but that may not be. For, his covenant is a covenant of grace; and the Lord who is free will not stand bent to thy bow, or give thee grace when thou wilt; for, it is not for us *Wait for* to know the times and seasons. What *mercy.* if the Lord will not give thee grace this year, nor the next, nor all thy life? If at the last gasp he will drop in a little of his favour, it is more than he owes thee. Therefore hear to day, and wait to morrow, and continue in so doing, because thou knowest not when God may bless his own ordinances. Complain not of delays, but wait, for God hath waited for you long; and therefore if he make you wait for peace of conscience, and assurance of his love, he deals but equally with you, and as shall be best with you. God gives what, and when, and how he will; therefore wait for it.

3. Know and consider, that thou hast rested upon thine own duties and *Rest not* endeavours, and so doest not go to *upon du-* God, that blesseth both the means, *ties.* and all the endeavours of his this way.

The fault therefore is thine own, (I say) thine own, because thou restest in thine own performances, and in the power of the means that thou apprehendest; and doest not go to God, that would have wrought more than all they can.   For, did a man depend upon God's power and mercy in his ordinances, he would always find some proportionable succour, as well when he finds no success, as when he finds any.   God sometimes gives, and sometimes delays to give.   But God's love is as constant when he gives not, as when he gives.   Therefore labour to quit all carnal confidence in holy duties.   Rest not in thine own performances, but look beyond all duties to God in Christ, and desire him to give thee the success above them.

Watch how thy soul behaves itself after the naked discharge of a duty.   All quiet and calm, notwithstanding he lives in a daily course and practice of sin ; so that he prays and lies, fasts and cozens, and yet this makes all whole : I tell you, it is an undoubted argument, that the soul did place a carnal confidence in his own performances, and as yet never attained to a Lord Christ in the duty.   For he that seeks a Saviour in his duties, and rests not in self-performances, this man brings a Saviour, a Christ into his soul.   And mark what follows ; Christ brings pardoning virtue, and purging virtue with him, and gives him more power against corruptions, and more suspicion over his own soul than ever he had before. So that the soul begins to quarrel with itself and lies down with shame, and says, what shall I think of my praying and hearing? Where is the virtue and power of it? Did ever Christ hear my prayers, or come into my soul by his ordinances? Where is the purging virtue then, to clear me of my sins? Where is the purifying virtue to cleanse me of my corruptions? This is a ground of a gracious heart, that placeth not any confidence in holy duties, but only in the Lord Christ.

Do not content yourselves in this, that you see a need of a Saviour, because your minds are enlightened therein, and your reason persuaded thereof; when in the mean time you place a kind of confidence in the duty performed and service discharged, and think thereby to bring Christ at your beck; and you in the mean while do what you please. This is a wonderful cunning craft of Satan. This I say then, a man may see a need of a Saviour; but do not quiet thy soul because thou knowest it must be so, and because thou findest by experience thou canst not help thyself, the guilt of sin still sticks upon thee, and therefore a Saviour now must help thee. I say content not thyself with the mere notion of it, to say, I see it should be so, and it must be so, and rest thyself contented in the performance of services, and think to bring a Saviour at thy beck, to do what thou wilt for thy soul : this is a slight that Satan has pinned to thy soul. Many think to have a sovereign authority over Christ, when they have performed duties : so that the man does not use the means to be led to Christ, but he takes up his duties to be commanders of Christ, and that he may dispose of Christ for his own turn, so that he makes Christ an abettor of his own wickedness, not a subduer of his corruptions. This is a marvellous deceit, when men rest in their own abilities, and so abuse Christ. And this will appear in these particulars.

First. Watch how thy heart is in the performance of duty. Doth thy prayer, and hearing, and performing of services, make thee venturous and fool-hardy to meddle with corruptions ? Then it is a certain ground thou placest carnal confidence in thine own performances. As for example : if a professor should say, what if I do now and then sin ? And what if I do now and then pilfer, and use false weights and measures ? I'll but pray so much the more, and fast so much the oftener. Will not my conscience then be satisfied ? It shall be satisfied ; I will command it : I will put in bail for my sin, and pray against it. Now I beseech you observe it ; this praying and performing of duties, is merely to command a Saviour to give allowance to sin, that so he may

commit it freely.   As who would say, I have authority over my Saviour, and he shall pardon my
sin, and give me allowance to commit sin.   O the
wretched villany that is in this man's heart !
Fearful is thy estate, whosoever thou art, that
makest thy performances an abettor of thy distempers : so that thou doest thy duties not to convey Christ, that he may help thee to prevent sin,
but that Christ may take off the venom and indignation of sin, that so thou mayest commit wickedness without either suspicion or further distrac-
tion.

Many a man makes his services his saviours ;
for, he makes them the bottom to bear up his
conscience.   The ground whereof is this : haply
he finds and feels by woful experience what the
fruits of sin are : he sees the venom of his corruptions, and the lamentable effects of all his sinful practices.   He thought it before a fine thing to
swear, and lie, and drink, and follow base company ; but now they are gravel to his heart, and gall
to his soul.   His conscience flieth in his face,
and he is ready to sink down to hell under the
burden of his mis-ordered life.   Conscience saith,
" these be thy sins, and these will be thy damna-
tion : they have been thy delight, but they will
prove thy shame and confusion in the end ; and
shortly thou shalt find the smart of them : to hell
therefore, be packing, and gone."

Now this man hath no other cure for his conscience in such a case, but this; he entreats conscience to be quiet. He confesseth he hath lived in base courses, and his condition to be very miserable; but now he will reform all. He hath neglected prayer heretofore, but now he will pray. He hath hated God's servants, but now he will love them. His ways have been exceeding evil, but now he will reform them, and now he will turn over a new leaf. This he saith, and this he thinks will serve his turn. And thus many poor souls use the means as mediators, and so fall short of Christ. But a gracious heart doth not only pray, and hear, and receive, and use all possible means to obtain Christ, but is restless and unsatisfied till he enjoy and possess Christ in the means. He rests not upon the bare performance of any duty, neither thinks by virtue of any such his endeavours to get into Christ.

I will express this particular more fully in this manner. A rich userer that is sick of some disease, tell him such a physician can cure him; but he stands upon state, and will not come without a great deal of charge. Charge, saith he, I do not stand upon that; I have money enough by me, enough to fetch him hither. Such a man now placeth all his confidence in his money. So when the soul sees the guilt of sin is not removed, and that conscience is still snarling, and that, the law condemning him, Christ is the only Saviour, and he only that can satisfy and cure all. But now, how shall Christ be procured? Why, his prayer, and fasting, and performances, may command so much, and that by the power and merit of the work done. The voice of a Pharisee, and proper language of a Papist. But what promise is there for it? Within-book none. But thus fools rest on their own performances, and so fall short of Christ and salvation.

Object. But oh! saith a poor sinner, fain would I go out of myself. I see too well now, that I have rested, and do rest upon duties done; but I cannot deny myself as I would.

I answer, it is Satan's subtilty to keep us in ourselves, by endeavouring thus to make us go out of ourselves. For by our own strength he would have us to do it; and persuades us we may. But this is a marvellous deepness of his, wherein he shews both malice and cunning in the superlative. For here he makes us believe (and we, out of ignorance are pursuaded as he would have us,) that we have the staff in our own hands; that is, the power to get out of ourselves. But is it so? Oh no! it is a supernatural work to be quite out of ourselves. The same hand must bring us out of ourselves, that must bring us to Christ. And this is self-denial. And self-

Self-denial,   denial is, when the soul knoweth it
what it is.   hath nothing, and therefore is so
                overpowered with the mighty hand
of God, and the work of his spirit, that it doth
not so much as expect any power or ability from
itself, or from the creature, in the doing of any
good.   For it knows it is dead, and therefore cannot help itself, much less can the creature do it
any good.   It therefore looks up to heaven, and
seeks all sufficiency from God alone.   For, observe, whiles I thus think that I have ability to
go out of myself; do I not then say, I have a
principle within me to deny myself?   But it is
not so ; rather it is quite contrary.   For to deny
a man's self, is to know he hath no power in himself to do any spiritual duty.   Therefore we must
look only to the voice that calleth us, the voice of
Christ, and know that he that calls us from the
ways of darkness, and out of ourselves, must and
will bring us out.   Therefore expect only power
from Christ to pluck thee out of thyself, and to
make thee a believer ; for the same hand must do
both, or it will never be.

I would not have a poor creature think thus
with himself : " If this means, and these ordinances will do me no good, nor work upon my
heart, I shall never have comfort."   But speak
thus unto God, and say, " in truth, Lord, I ex-

pect no power from myself, nor from the means ; but my resolution is, to look up to him that hath hid his face yet from his poor servant. I will not look any lower, as here within myself, for any such power : no, Lord, but to the highest in power and gifts. Nor will I look to the minister, or to the means, but I will wait upon thee, O Lord, and look up to thy power, to work by thine own means." Remember what the prophet saith : Isaiah, 50, 10. *Who is among you that feareth the Lord, and obeyeth the voice of his servant, that walketh in darkness, and hath no light, let him trust in the name of the Lord, and stay himself upon his God.* Then when all other things in the world fail, let the soul look up to the Lord, and get away from itself. For then is the fittest time of all to meet with God. I would have a Christian choose this time above all times, the fittest wherein to meet his Saviour, and to disappoint Satan. For, as I said, it is the last refuge that the devil hath : and if he miss of this, his force is gone forever. For otherwise the sinner, partly seeing the beauty of grace, will not ; and partly seeing the baseness of his own heart, will not dare to come to Christ.

3. But the next complaint, is, want of sense and feeling, such as a Christian must have, and finds not. Therefore the distressed soul saith, " alas ! I never knew what it was to have the

assurance of God's love; I never received any evidence of God's favour; and can I then think that I have faith? They that believe, have their hearts filled with joy unspeakable and glorious; the word saith as much: but I am a stranger to this joy; how then can I think that I have any work of faith wrought in me?"

I answer; this doth not hinder, either that thou hast not faith, or that thou mayest not come to God in Christ by believing. Only remember these three particulars:

First; thou must not think to have this joy and refreshing before thou goest to the promise.— Thou must look for it when thou hast chewed and fed upon it. Or wouldest thou have the Lord give thee the whole bargain at once, and before the match be made? This joy is a fruit that proceeds from faith after much wrestling; and doth not presently flow from faith, not so soon as ever a Christian begins to believe, but after a time; and then the heart is joyous; but never filled with joy before believing. Afterwards, and when a man hath had the sweet dew of the promises dropping upon him, but many a day after, let him look for this joy.

Secondly; know that these joys, and this sense and feeling may be absent from faith. For a man may have a good faith, and yet want the relish and sweetness which he longs after. One may want what he desires, and yet want neither life nor heat. A tree may want leaves and fruit, and yet want neither sap nor moisture. And a man's faith may be somewhat strong, when his feeling is nothing at all. David was justified and sanctified, and yet wanted this joy. And Job trusted upon God when he had but little feeling; as when he saith, *thou makest me a but to shoot at; yet I will trust in thee though thou kill me.* Therefore build not your comfort upon sense and feeling, which is to build upon the sand; but go to the promise, as to the rock, for it.

Quest. But how comes this desire after Christ?

I answer : there are no more but two affections in the soul to absent good, God infinitely wise having so framed it; and these two are hope and desire. The understanding says, such a thing is profitable and comfortable if I had it. Then hope is sent out to wait for that goodness. And if it comes not, then desire is sent out to meet that goodness. Hope stands and waits for it, but desire wanders up and down seeking and inquiring after a Lord Jesus, and goes from coast to coast, from east to west ; " O that I could, O that I might, and when shall I ? And how may I come to the speech of a Lord Christ ?" As it was with the spouse in the Canticles; when her beloved was gone, she wandered up and down seeking him, and inquiring of the watchmen if they did not see

him whom her soul loved ; so she wanders from
this thing to that, from this place to that place, and
never ceaseth to seek and see if she can gain notice of Christ.   It goes to prayer, to see if that
will entreat a Christ.   It goes to the word, to see
if that will reveal a Christ.   It goes to conference,
to see if it can hear of Christ there.   Then it
comes to the congregation, and to the sacrament,
to see if it can hear of any news of a Lord Christ,
and of mercy.

The soul thus continues wandering and seeking, till at last the Lord Christ comes into the
soul, when the soul hath thus hungered and long-
ed for him.   At length the Lord Christ is pleased
to shew himself : *Behold, the King cometh :* so
the soul says, *Behold the Lamb of God, that
takes away thy sins.*   O thou poor broken-hearted
sinner, here is thy Saviour ; he is come down
from heaven to speak peace to thy soul in the
pardon of thy sins.   Thou that hungerest for a
Christ, here he is to satisfy thee.   Thou that
thirsteth after Christ, here he is to refresh thee.
Thou that hast long sought him, he saith, " here I
am, and all my merits are thine."

Now when the Lord Jesus is pleased to present
himself to the soul, desire hath met with the
Lord.

It is in this case with a sinner, as it is with a
traitor who is pursued, and takes a strong hold,

and is there besieged. And now he seeth no
hope of favour, nor hope of escape. Therefore he
is content to submit, and lay his head on the
block, that he may receive punishment for his
offence. Now coming to execution, he hears an
inkling from the messenger there is yet hope he
may be pardoned. The poor traitor in the prison,
with that is stirred up to hope. Nay, then he
hears by another messenger from the king himself, if he will come to the court, and seek to his
majesty, and importune his grace for mercy and
favour, it is like he shall be pardoned. Then he
makes haste, and desire carries him to the court
to sue for favour from the king. So that now he
will be listening and inquiring of every one there,
" Did you hear the king speak nothing of me ?
How stands the king's mind towards me ? Pray
how goes my case ?" Then some tell him, " the
truth is, the king hears you are humbled, and
that you are sorry for what you have done." At
last the king looks out of the window, and sees
the malefactor, and says, " is this the traitor ?"
One says, " yes, if it please your highness, this is
the man that is humbled and pleads for mercy,
and desires nothing so much as favour." Hereupon, the king being full of mercy, tells him, " the
truth is, his pardon is drawing, and coming towards him." With that his heart leaps in his
bowels, and is enlarged towards his majesty ; and

he says, " God bless your majesty; never was there so favourable a prince to so poor a traitor." His heart leaps for joy, because his pardon is coming towards him. Haply it is not sealed yet: now when it is sealed, and all done, the king calls him in, and delivers it.

So it is with a poor sinner, he is the malefactor. You that have committed high treason, you think not of it: but take heed, God will pursue you one day. Haply God lets you alone for the present, but he will surprise you on a sudden, and conscience will pluck thee by the throat, and carry thee down to hell. And now the Lord pursues him with a heavy stroke and indignation, and lets fly at his face, and sets conscience at work as a pursuivant, and that says ; " these are thy sins, and to hell thou must go ; God hath sent me to execute thy soul." Now the poor soul sees he can no way escape from the Lord, and to purchase any favour he sees it impossible ; therefore he is resolved to lie down at God's feet, and hope. Now hope is a faculty of the soul to look out for mercy. As a man that is in expectation of the coming of his friend, goeth to the top of a hill, looks round about him, to see if he can understand any thing of his friend ; so the soul hopes and waits, and stretches itself out for mercy. " When will it be, Lord ? When will this pardon come ?" The soul gets up and stands as it were a tip-toe : " O when will it come, Lord ?"

How does God stir up the heart to hope ? It is worth the while to consider how this is maintained.

1. The Lord sweetly stays the heart, and persuades it that his sins are pardonable, and that the good he wants may be supplied; this is a great support to the soul. Hope is always expectation of a good to come. Now when a poor sinner sees his sins, the number of them, the nature of them, the vileness of them, the cursedness of his soul, that he can take no rest; he sees no rest in the creature, nor in himself. Though he pray all day, yet he cannot get the pardon of one sin. The soul is out of any expectation of pardon, or power of mercy in any thing he hath or doth. Though all means, all helps, though all men and angels should join together, yet they cannot pardon one sin of his. Now the Lord lifts up his voice, and says from heaven, "thy sins are pardonable." O the infiniteness of God's power! though the guilt of sin is powerful to condemn the soul. But when the infinite power of the Lord is considered, as able to overpower all his sins, this lifteth up the heart in some expectation that the Lord will show mercy to a man; though it is a hard thing to hope, when the soul is thus troubled. " Can this heart be broken ? Can these sins be

pardoned ? Can this soul be saved ?" Now
comes in the power of God : God can pardon
them. Never measure the power of God by that
shallow conceit of thine. All things are possible
to God, though not to men. And as it is said of
Abraham, he hoped above hope ; he looked to
the Lord that was able to do what he had promised : he considered not that he had a dead body,
but that he had a living God to hope on. Justice
cannot be so severe to revenge thee, as mercy is
gracious to do good unto thee. If thy sins be
never so many, God's justice never so great ; yet
mercy is above all thy sins, above all thy rebel-
lions. This may support thy soul.

So here you have the first ground to stir up
hope; thy sins are pardonable. There is more
power in God to show mercy to thee, than power
in sin to destroy thee.

The Lord Jesus Christ came to seek and to
save that which was lost. It was the scope of
his coming. Now saith the broken and humble
sinner, "I am lost. Did Christ come to save
sinners ? Then Christ must fail of his end, or I
of my comfort. God says, *come to me all ye that
are weary and heavy laden :* I am weary : unless
the Lord intended good to me, why did he invite
me, and bid me come ? Surely he means to show
mercy to me."

Oh take heed of despair. Question thy estate

thou mayest, thou must; but to cast away all hope is very heinous in the eyes of the Lord. Cast away all carnal confidence thou must, and yet thou must hope. *Let Israel hope in the Lord: for with the Lord there is mercy, and with him is plenteous redemption.*

The Lord takes this very ill at our hands. Thou goest to the deep dungeon of thy corruption, and there thou sayest " these sins can never be pardoned : I am still proud, and more stubborn : this distress God seeth not, God succoureth not, his hand cannot reach, his mercy cannot save." Now mark what the prophet saith to such a perplexed soul, Isaiah 40, 27, *Why sayest thou my way is hid from the Lord!* The Lord saith, why sayest thou so? *The young men shall faint and be weary ; but they that wait on the Lord shall renew their strength.* Is any thing too hard for the Lord? You wrong God exceedingly : You think it is matter of humility, to count yourself so vile. Can God pardon such a wretch's sin as mine ? Mark that place of the Psalmist ; they spake against the Lord, *can the Lord prepare a table in the wilderness?* They spake not against themselves, but against the Lord. So we speak against God, and charge God himself. "It is true," says the soul, " Manasseh was pardoned, Paul was converted, God's saints have been received to mercy ; but can my sin be pardoned?

Can my soul be quickened? No, no, my sins are greater than can be pardoned," saith the despairing soul. Consider how injurious this is to God, to make the power of sin greater to condemn thee, than the power of God to save thee: to make the power of Satan stronger to ruin thee than the power of God to relieve thee, and succour thee. And what can you say more? And what can you do more against the Lord? Is not this to make God an underling to Satan, and to sin? This is just as to say, the Almightiness of God is weaker than the weakness of sin; the sufficiency of God is weaker than the malice of Satan. It is so; poor humble sinners many times will make bitter complaints this way; and they think they speak against themselves. No, no, they speak against the Lord. They spake against the Lord, when they said, *can the Lord prepare a table in the wilderness?* So you speak in this desperate manner: "why truth, Lord, this proud heart will never be humbled; if any thing would have wrought, it would have been done ere this day. How many sermons, how many mercies, how many judgments, how many prayers? And yet this proud heart, this stubborn heart will not be reformed." You think you speak against yourselves now: no, no, you speak against the Lord. And know, this is one of the greatest sins thou committest, to say thy sins cannot be forgiven.

2. As this sin is injurious to God, so it is dangerous to thy own soul. It is that which takes up the bridge, and cuts off all passages, and there can no spiritual comfort or consolation come into the soul of a poor sinner. Luke 3, 5, 6. *Every valley* (or ditch) *shall be filled, and then all flesh shall see the salvation of the Lord.* What are these ditches? Why nothing else but those deep gulfs and ditches of despair: and unless they be filled, no man can see the Lord Jesus Christ. The truth is, this despair of the soul is that which cuts the sinews of man's comfort, and takes off the power and edge of all the means of grace; daunts all a man's endeavours; nay, it plucks up endeavours by the very roots: for that which a man despairs of, he will never labour after. It is here, as with a man in the pangs of death: unto such a man, as all things are unavailable for his good; his bed will not ease him, meat will not refresh him, chafing will not revive him; at last we say he is gone, he is a dead man. Friends leave him, physicians leave him. They may go and pray for him, and mourn for him, but they cannot recover him. So this despair of soul makes a man cast off all hope, and lie down in a forlorn condition, expecting no good to come. "Alas," saith the poor soul, "what skilleth for a man to pray? What profiteth it a man to read? What benefit in all the means of grace? The

truth is, the stone is rolled upon me, and my condemnation is sealed forever, and therefore I will
never look after Christ, grace and salvation any
more." Let him come to hear the word, and
mark how he casts off the benefit of it. It was
marvellous, seasonable and profitable, it was the
good word of God unto such as have share therein : why then may not you expect benefit there-
from ? " No," saith the soul, " the time of grace
is past, the day is gone." If ministers would
pray for him, and good people pray for him, he
bids them save their labour ; for hell is his portion, and his condemnation is sealed in heaven.
See now and consider what desperate danger despair brings to a poor heart, and carries him beyond the reach of mercy. That's a sweet passage of David's, Psalm 77, 7. *Will the Lord
cast off for ever ? I said this is my infirmity.*
The word in the original, *this is my sickness,* as
who shall say, " this would be my death : what,
is mercy gone for ever ? then my life is gone,
then is all my comfort gone, my hope gone :"
therefore take heed of this, it takes off the edge of
all our endeavours and God's ordinances that
might do us good.

3. This marvellously condemns that great sin
of presumption ; a sin more frequent, and if it be
possible, more dangerous ; the presumption of
carnal hypocrites that bolster themselves up with

marvellous boldness in their course. It is as true here, and I beseech you observe it, as they said *Saul hath slain his thousands, and David his ten thousands :* despair hath slain his thousands, but presumption his ten thousands; that men may swear, and lie, and cozen, and break all commands, and yet hope to be saved. They hope grace will save them, and yet resist grace. They hope Jesus Christ will save them, and yet oppose Christ. This is that which hath slain many thousands among us ; and they are few that have not split upon this rock. And therefore I say, this serves to reprove the baseness of such hypocrites as boast themselves, and compare their hopes with the hopes of the saints. " It is true," say they, " I cannot walk so freely, I cannot repeat a sermon, I have not those parts that they have ; yet I hope to be saved as well as they." This is that which hath slain so many thousands of souls that are now roaring in hell ; they may thank presumption for it.

Now this hope is not the hope of the saints. The hope of the saints is a grounded hope ; but these hopes hang upon some idle pleas and foolish pretences, and some carnal reasons. But I tell you they will fail, and sink into the bottomless pit ere they are aware. It is the command and counsel of Peter, *that every man should be ready to give an account of his faith and hope that is in him.* Look to the reasons that carry you, and to the arguments that persuade you; see they be not groundless and foolish hopes. You hope to be saved, and you hope to go to heaven, and you hope to see the face of God with comfort. Look about, I say; good hope hath good reason, grounded hope grounded reason.

4. The saints of God many times are deprived of comfort, not because God withholds it, but because they put it from themselves, and will not have it, though he offered it; as David, Psalm 77. *My soul refused comfort.* He was a sullen child that will not eat his milk, because he cannot have it in the golden dish. So sometimes, and because God doth not for us what we would, we will have nothing at all. These are the main hinderances, and I might add many more; for carnal reason is very fruitful this way; and we through our own folly, and the devil's craft, are apt to abuse things, and to make them hinderances in our way to happiness eternal.

CHAPTER II

Helps to come to Christ

I COME now to the cures of all these impediments, where, if we had the wisdom and care we should have, we might break through them all to Christ. The means especially are four, whereby we may be inwardly strengthened against them all, and be at last able to overcome, and put them to foil for ever.

The first cure and help is this ; we must not look too long, nor pore too much, or unwarrantably upon our own corruptions within, so far as to be disheartened by them from coming to the riches of God's grace. For this is a sure and everlasting truth, that whatsoever sight of sin unfits a man for mercy, when he may take it, and it is offered ; that sight of sin is ever sinful, though it have never so fair an outside of sorrow and deep humiliation. Namely, as when we think, and say, (as often we do,) had I a soul so thoroughly humbled, and bruised, and softened, and so forth, I could do well enough. And thus the devil keeps us in sin by poring too long *The godly* and much upon our sins; as thinking *sorrow* thereby to get from them. But such *what it is.*

a course is a sinful course. Tell not me of sorrow, and repentance, and humiliation ; all that sorrow, and humiliation, and repentance, is naught, that keeps a man from receiving mercy when there is need, and it is offered. See this in Abraham, he had this promise, that he should have a son in his old age : and Rom. 4, 19. *He being not weak in faith, regarded not his old age or deadness, nor the barrenness of Sarah's womb, but believed in him who had promised it.* There he rests, and there he stays ; he saw his body was dead, yet there was a living promise ; and what though Sarah's womb was barren, yet the promise was fruitful. He knew his own deadness and her barrenness ; but he stood not long there. As Abraham therefore, so we may see our sins, and consider our many weaknesses ; but must not so settle upon them, or consider of them so as to be hindered by them from coming to God for mercy, which he freely offers us, and we stand in need of. For, while the soul of a man is daily plodding upon his own misery and distempered life, these two things follow.

1. Stop the stream of God's promise, and let down the sluice against it, so that the promise cannot enter into us.

2. We set open the stream and flood-gate of corruption, and make it to run most violently down, and to flood in upon us ; and in the end to

ovewhelm us. Now the inconvenience arising
hereby, is enough to flay the best Christian in the
world ; for what can a man get out of his corruption ? He can have no more thereof than is to be
had ; and it is in vain to look for comfort where
it is not to be had. All this, and the least of all
this may dishearten us, but will not encourage
us, or put heart into us. See the humility and
wisdom of the woman of Canaan, Matthew 15, 17.
She follows Christ ; but he listens not to her, but
gives her a sore foil, and calls her dog ; and saith,
" you Gentiles are dogs ; and the gospel of grace
and salvation is the children's bread." Now if
she had only considered the words of Christ, and
only looked into herself and her own baseness,
she had never come to have received either mercy
or comfort from him. But she saith, " *truth
Lord, I am a dog, yet the dogs eat of the crumbs
that fall from their master's table.*" This was
her resolution. Wherein there are two things
which express and set forth the frame of a gracious heart ; a heart that is truly wise to attend
to its own baseness, with faith : and that is her
humility and wisdom. As if she had said, " thou
sayest I am a Gentile and a dog ; I confess it :"
there's her humility. " Yet though I am a dog, I
will not go out of doors, but lie under the table
for mercy :" there is her wisdom. And thus she ;
and so we must. And when our corruptions, as

I said, flood in upon us, and we see ourselves quite lost, and damned in our sins, we must then say, " in truth Lord, I am as bad as thy word can make me, yet let me not fly from mercy, but lie at the feet of my Saviour's mercy, till he look upon me as once upon Peter, Luke 22, 61.

It is fit, and we ought to see our sins : but stay we must not too long there. See them we must, but not fasten on them, so as to shackle us from coming to Christ. I have said it, and will say it, that that sight of sin which doth not drive a man to Christ for mercy, is ever sinful. Labour therefore to see thy sins, and that thus ;

First ; see thy sins in the royal law, as in the right glass ; a glass that will present them such as they be, and look not off till thou hast seen them so.

Secondly ; so see them, as that by such a holy gaze at them, thou mayest see an utter insufficiency in thyself to satisfy for them.

Thirdly ; and so see them, that thou mayest by that sight behold an absolute necessity of Christ to succour thee, and then away speedily to him that can only help thee, and dwell no longer on thy sins, but go to the throne of grace, where is plentiful redemption, whence issue out pardons in abundance to remove that guilt that sin hath brought upon thy soul ; and where is power enough to enable thee to be more than conqueror over thy corruption. Briefly, every soul should say thus ; " it is true, Lord, my sins are many and great, for I have departed from thee the fountain of bliss : but shall I go on, and so further from thee, and persist in evil ? God forbid." All this while I speak to broken-hearted Christians. You profane ones, you have your portion already, and shall have more of it in hell hereafter ; therefore for a while stand you by, and let the children come to their bread.

Isaiah 66, 2. *The Lord looks to him that is of an humble and contrite heart, and that trembleth at his word.* A poor creature cannot but observe every word of God, and tremble at every truth ; whose meditation is such as this : " here is salvation indeed but it is not mine ; here is mercy, but I have no part in so great mercy ;" and thus he shakes at every apprehension of every word of God, concluding certainly that he shall never enjoy any part of it. But mark what the text saith, *the Lord looks at such a trembling soul ;* that is, he casts sweet intimations of his goodness and love into him, and saith, " thou poor trembling sinner, to thee be it spoken, I have an eye toward thee in the Lord Jesus Christ." Therefore he further saith, Isaiah 40, 2. *Comfort ye, comfort ye my people, speak comfortably to Jerusalem, and cry unto her, that her warfare is accomplished, and her iniquity is pardoned:* " tell

Jerusalem she is accepted, tell her what my mind is."

And here he goes on, and saith to his minister, "speak to the heart of such an humble penitent, and tell him from me, nay tell him from heaven, and tell him from the Lord Jesus Christ, and from under the hand of the Spirit, that his person is accepted, and his sins are all of them done away, and he himself shined upon in great mercy."

Here Ephraim is the picture of a soul truly humbled, in whose behaviour we may see the behaviour of a true penitent towards God; and God's dealing towards him. The text saith, Jer. 31, 18, 19, 20. *Surely I have heard Ephraim bemoaning himself* (there's the heart broken and thirsty) *thou hast chastised me, and I was chastised; turn thou me, and I shall be turned; thou art the Lord my God. Surely after that I was turned, I repented, and after that I was instructed, I smote upon my thigh; I was ashamed, yea, even confounded, because I did bear the reproach of my youth.* Thus the sinner, as if he should have said, "I am the wretch that have seen all the means of grace in an abundant measure, and yet never profited under the hand of any. The Lord hath corrected me, but I would not be tamed; and he instructed me, but I would not learn. Lord turn me, thou art my God; I have nothing in myself; nav, now I see the evils

which before I never perceived ; and I observe
the baseness of my course, which before I considered not. Now I am ashamed of my abuse of
grace so plainly revealed : I am even now confounded with the sense of those abominations my
soul did formerly take pleasure in." This may
be conceived to be the mourning of a poor and
much broken sinner. And now mark God's answer : *Ephraim is my Son, he is a pleasant child :
for since I spake against him, I do earnestly remember him still, therefore my bowels are troubled
for him, I will surely have mercy upon him.* As
much as to say ; "I observed all those secret
sighs, I considered all those tears, I heard all
those prayers, and took notice of all those complaints, and my bowels even yearn towards this
poor dejected sinner, an humble soul that seeks
to me for mercy. The truth is ; I will embrace
him with my loving kindness." This for the
first help.

Now, the second means of cure is this, take
heed of judging thy estate by carnal reason without the rule ; which is commonly the fashion and
fault of poor distressed spirits, who pass fearful
sentence against themselves upon groundless arguments, and say, " I never found it, I feel no
such thing, and I fear it is not so." But in this
we hear but carnal pleas, coming out of Satan's
forge, and by his help, from ourselves, against

ourselves, for we judge ourselves by them. But,
I say, take heed of this wile of
The danger of Satan's, and make conscience of
judging our- this as much as of any other
selves rashly. fault, as much as of swearing,
stealing, adultery, or murder;
for it is as truly sin as those, though not so great;
yet a far greater sin than you imagine. Consider
this thou humble-hearted Christian, for to thee I
speak. Therefore when upon these grounds thou
concludest that thy case and estate is naught, see
and consider against how many commandments
thou offendest.

First, thou dishonourest God, and the work of
his grace, by denying that which God hath done
for thee. Also, and speakest unreverently against
him. Besides, thou art a murderer, for that thou
woundest thine own soul. Further, thou robbest
thyself of much comfort, and so art a thief. And
thou barest false witness against thyself, yea,
against Christ, and the spirit of Christ, and the
work of grace already wrought in thee. Also
thou joinest with the devil against the Lord Jesus
Christ. Are these no sins?

You will say, " I speak as I think." Yet that
hinders not but that thou bearest false witness.
As we see, if a man affirm such an one is a drunkard, and knows it not, this man bears false witness;
because though the man be indeed a drunkard,

yet it is more than he knows. So thou sayest thou hast nothing, when thou dost but only fear it, and suspect it, and dost not feel it. I speak this the rather, because of the sinful distemper that creeps in upon the hearts of many broken-hearted Christians ; and so as that out of a self-willed road of carnal reason, and a vile haunt that they have gotten, their hearts are persuaded that they do well to do so, and that they can never be well except they do so.

But they that are such, (mark what I say,) when reason is plain against them, and plain Scripture evidenceth the contrary, do not so much attend what the minister saith, as they stand and invent, how they may answer the minister ; and so put away their own mercy. Therefore let the fear of God fall upon every poor soul that heareth this ; and let him know, that however he hath taken or given leave to himself, or taken up the wasters, by taking up pleas against the truth ; yet now he is to change the course, to go aside, and to mourn apart for his misprision : also to wonder that the Lord hath not all this while taken away all the comforts of his grace, and all the motions of his Spirit from him. The prophet David prays the Lord to *turn away his eyes from beholding vanity*, Psalm 119, 37. Now if God must do that ; that is, turn away our eyes that they see not ; much more must he turn away our hearts that they attend not on lying vanities. We must attend God and the voice of his Spirit ; but to listen to carnal pleas, (which we have no warrant to do,) is to sin deeply, and to hurt our own soul both deeply and dangerously. No man would deal with a cheater. Carnal reason is a cheater, therefore we should not heed it, unless we would resolve to be cozened. And now if the danger of the sin cannot make us to do this ; let the sorrow that will come of it, constrain us. The prophet saith, Isaiah 50, 11. *Behold, all you that kindle a fire, and that compass yourselves about with the sparks that ye have kinkled ; this shall ye have at my hand, ye shall lie down in sorrow.* These are the prophet's words ; nay, God's by him. And now I will tell you what is meant by sparks, and what by fire. In the old law, as some of you know, there was heavenly fire kept continually upon the altar of the sanctuary, which shadowed out the will and wisdom of God in his word ; and there was also strange fire, that is divers sparkles of men's own imaginations and conceits. Concerning this, every poor creature carries his tinder-box about him, and is ever kindling of it. But such a fire much provoked God once, and so doth still. So saith the text ; in which are two things. First, that the heart of man will naturally invent carnal reasons and pleas against itself, and be settled upon them as upon the dregs of a vessel that is at bottom. Secondly, that the issue that followeth is fearful ; for it is said, *this shall ye have of mine hand, ye shall lie down in sorrow.* Now then, when the Scriptures are clear, and reasons upon it evident, yet you will have your own devices and ways; thus much I must tell you, *you shall lie down in sorrow* at last, and you may thank yourselves for it. Away then with your tinder-boxes; abase yourselves before the throne of grace, and be at last wise to salvation so nigh.

"*Ho, every one that thirsteth,* (saith God by his prophet,) *come and buy without money, take of the well of the water of life freely, and live forever.*" Many a poor minister, while he preaches the good word of God, would fain leave his commodity behind him, while he saith, " you must have it; and you shall have it ; it is your portion, and belongs of right unto you." Thus we are fain even to force God's favour upon you. Hereupon we beseech you to believe, and we entreat you for the Lord Jesus' sake to receive mercy, and to humble your hearts.

Thus we deal with you in fatherly terms. But will you take so great and so good a commodity from us ?

No, beloved ; many sweet promises, and many admirable precious things of grace and salvation are revealed, but men are negligent to take for themselves. In this case our markets stand upon ourselves ; we pass not to lay out any thing here to benefit : some carnal plea or other mars all. This argues plainly the small estimation that we have of Christ. But the poor hungry sinner, one that is apprehensive of his own weakness and feebleness, longs till the feast-day cometh, that he may partake of these and such delicates. Oh ! how carefully doth he listen, and how diligently doth he attend what the minister saith ? And if the word come home to his conscience, enlightening his heart, and reproving him of his ways : then he cries out ; " oh ! I am in great trouble ; good Lord comfort me : I am full of doubts ; good Lord resolve me : I am ignorant in spiritual things ; good Lord teach me : I have a proud, stout, stubborn heart ; good Lord humble me." He was never better than now. Therefore take this for a general rule ; that a good heart is never better at ease, than when the word works most, and most bitingly. Contrarily, a wicked graceless person is never better than when the word works least, or never a whit upon him. But when he thinks the minister will come close to his sore and soul, he will not be at home that day, he will be sure to be out of the town, or not in place. He knows the word would awaken him, and affright him, and he cannot bear the blow, therefore he keeps away, and shuns the hearing of the word, when it should work to his reformation any way.

And now for a third help, let us be marvellously wary and watchful that we enter not into the lists of, and dispute with Satan, upon points which are beyond the reach of man, as thus to say; " I am not elected, therefore God will not look upon me to do me any good. Or, it is a vain thing for me to use the means of mercy, my time of mercy being out. Oh! the days of grace that I have seen, when the Lord knocked sweetly at my heart, and was pleased to reveal my sins unto me at such a time : but then, hard-hearted wretch that I was, I shut the door upon him, and now he is gone and past ; and now there is no hope for the visit of grace, or that Christ should return again to show me any mercy." If the devil can have thee here, all thy comfort is gone ; for upon this ground a man shall never receive rest to his soul, come what days will. And how can he ? For if he cannot judge of, or know comfort, how shall I the minister, be able to give, or he, the hearer, to take it ?

And here look as it is with a poor travelling man, one that falleth among thieves, who come and promise to carry him a nearer way, but bring him into a wood whither no passengers come, and there they do what they will unto him. So it is with a poor soul, when the devil gets him into

these unwarranted disputes, as it were ; large
wildernesses of God's eternal counsel, where are
no passengers, and therefore he cannot but be void
of helps and succour, and so as that Satan may
now exercise his full pleasure, and whole malice,
by terrifying his poor desolate soul.

To avoid which straits, observe these three
rules.

First ; let the soul in this case bear upon the
Almightiness of the power of God, who said to
Abraham, *1 am God all-sufficient,* Gen. 17, 1.
For if thou be persuaded of the all-sufficiency of
God, that assurance cannot but stay thee slipping
from falling.   And here remember that God can
do more than thou canst think.   He is able, and
doth thee good, though thou know it not. And further, consider that the soul cannot doubt of God's
will, but with that very doubt makes some question of his power.   This for the first rule.

For the second.   It bids check thine own heart
for meddling with God's secrets, and for prying
so into his closet of hidden counsels.   For no
man should go beyond his bounds ; and it apper-
tains not to thee to look into this ark of matters
sealed up. Deut. 29, 29. *Secret things belong
to God, but revealed things belong to us.   And
who hath known the mind of God ?* saith Paul, 1
Cor. 2, 16.   Mark this, you that will be climbing
up the ladder of God's eternal predestination, and

going up into the skies to know what God's secret
mind is.   Keep your stations wisely; for neither
the devil, nor all the devils in hell, ever knew the
mind of the Lord.   When Jonah cried against
Nineveh, saying, within forty days all you; that
is, all you drunkards, and adulterers, and murder-
ers, and others, shall be destroyed : mark here
how the king resolves : Jonah 4, 19.   *Who can
tell if the Lord will repent, and stay his fierce
wrath that we perish not?*   Therefore the devil
tells thee thus much, and saith, "God hath appointed a way to salvation, and you have had the
means, and did not profit by them, therefore God
will never show you mercy, nor give you grace."
Thus the devil.   But how can he tell that?
Surely all the devils in hell cannot tell it.   Say
with thyself, "let me walk in that course which
God hath appointed and commanded, and do that
which I ought; and then I may say, and with
comfort say it, who knows but God may break
the heart of a proud, rebellious, contrary sinner,
such as mine is, and such as I am?"   None verily
but God knows whether or no.

Thirdly ; therefore measure not the riches of
God's love, and the sweetness of his saving grace
according to your own conceits ; nor do you think
that because you cannot conceive it, therefore
God will not do it, for the prophet saith, Isaiah

55, 7, 8, 9. *Let the wicked forsake his way,
and the unrighteous man his thoughts ;* that is, all
you wicked ones, and you that have lived lewdly,
return from your wicked ways, and vain thoughts,
and he will abundantly show mercy.

"But will the Lord pardon all my sins," saith
the poor doubting soul?   " I cannot think it : If
I myself were a God, I should never pass by such
intolerable things as have been done by me."

Because you cannot, you think God cannot or
will not.   Yes, saith the Lord, " *I can abundantly pardon : for my thoughts are not your thoughts,
nor my ways as your ways.*"   A poor creature
thinks his sins are unpardonable, and that he shall
never get assurance of God's favour, or hope of
his love.   "But you are men," saith the Lord,
" and have finite thoughts ; but I am a God, and
in mercies infinite, when you think I will have no
mercy."

"But were ever any such received to mercy as
I," saith the drooping soul?   "And therefore
why should I be the only man?"

To this I say : when Christ had wrought many
strange miracles, the people said there were never
any such things done in Israel.   And therefore it
is plain not to be doubted, that God can do things
that never like were done : Job 9, 10.   *He doth
great things past finding out, and wonders with-*

out number, saith Job: and therefore judge not either God's power or love by thy scantling.*

The best Christians are most suspicious of themselves, and none fuller of doubts and fears, than those that have least cause to fear or doubt that their estates are broken and bad. Therefore Satan makes it his chief work to grieve and terrify such. Besides, their own distrustful hearts are always ready to join issue with his false reports against them, raising false surmises against themselves, and putting mercy from them; as if they were hired by the devil to take his part in pleading against their own sure salvation. Therefore it is worth the time to hear what David saith, Psalm 42, 8. *The Lord shall command his loving-kindness in the morning*. It is a phrase taken from princes and great men, whose words are a law of command. For so God will send forth, as by a commandment, his loving-kindness to a truly humble Christian. As if it should be said : " go, love and everlasting mercy, take thy commission ; and I charge thee go to that poor broken-hearted sinner, go to that poor, hungry and thirsty soul : go and prosper, and prevail, and stamp my love upon his heart, and there let it stand whether he will or not." Thus the Lord charges his loving-kindness to do good to poor sinners, and by his own Almightiness bears up the soul, when it is

* Narrow views. Ed.

ready to sink under the weighty burden of its many transgressions.

"But what? Shall I have mercy? No, no, (saith the poor doubting heart.) Will the Lord Jesus accept me? No, surely. Could I pray so, and so, and had I these and those parts, and could I perform duties after this and that manner, then there were some hope; but all is contrary, and therefore wo and alas, there is no mercy for me."

But to answer this also, let me tell thee, whoever thou art, that God invites thee in particular, as by name; and that all the sweetness in Christ, and in his precious promises appertain to thy soul, and thou hast as great an interest in them as any servant of God in the world whatsoever.

"No, no," saith the trembling soul, "I cannot believe that such a wretch as I, shall, or can go to heaven. It cannot be. Heaven shall rather fall than I come there." Thus the discouraged sinner knocks for mercy, and shuts the door against himself.

And now, when all carnal reasonings, and high soaring imaginations, as Paul calls them, have raised up strong holds against mercy and comfort; when the word cannot for the present settle peace in the unquiet soul; God is made at last to command his loving-kindness, and send it with a commission from heaven; and to say unto it, "I charge you break open the doors of such a reluctant sinner, rend off that veil of ignorance that is before his eyes ; silence all his doubts and fears. And when this is done, I charge you go home to that broken soul, and cheer and refresh it with the sense of my sweet favour ; and with the assurance of my love to fill it."

While we were enemies, saith the apostle, *Christ died for us*, Rom. 5, 8.   And here the Lord sends from heaven to a poor miserable creature, and saith, " commend my love, commend my mercy to such a distressed soul, and tell it, though it hath been an enemy to me, yet I am a friend to it. Tell it, though it hath been a traitor to me, I have been a good king to it.   And tell it, that though it hath been a rebel to me, I have yet been a loving God to it.   Tell the man, whose heart that is, that his sins are pardoned, his person accepted, and that his soul shall be saved.   Tell him his sighs and groans are not lost, and that his prayers are heard in heaven.   Let him know that the Lord Jesus died for sinners when they were sinners.   Make all this good to his soul, I charge you before you come back."

The fourth cure is this.   And it is especially to be observed by a Christian above all, in his proceedings with himself in bar of judgment ; and that is, pass no hasty sentence against thyself but according to the evidence of the word.   If thou art to be approved, let the word of God do it : and

let the same word examine thee, if thou comest
to be examined.   If this word speak for thee, no
matter, though all men and angels speak against
thee, and if it condemn thee, no matter who
speaks for thee : by it thou risest or fallest to
thine own master.   What though some wrangling
fellow step in, and will be determining causes before the judge comes : shall his word stand ? No.
Therefore a wise man will stay till the judge himself do come, and wait upon the judgment of his
mouth.   Deal thou no otherwise with thine own
soul : put not the case to be tried by a company
of peevish carnal reasons, but stay till the word,
(which is the judge,) come ; and judge thyself by
that, and hold to that for thy life, and the life of
thy soul.   *The light is that which manifesteth all
things*, saith the apostle, Eph. 4, 13.   His meaning is : the light of the word, and the evidence of
God's truth, manifested to the souls of God's
people ; these properly are the judges.   The other
are but wrangling cases, not to be admitted.   And
here sense and feeling, grounded upon carnal matter, are like fogs and mists, which make a man
that he cannot see his way, but upon clearing up
his state and condition, it is open before him ;
and then it is manifest what it is.   *Learn of me*,
saith our Saviour, Mat. 11, 29, *and you shall
find rest to your souls*.   And the Psalmist saith ;
I will inquire what the Lord will say.   So say

thou, " I will not hearken what carnal reason will say; I will hear what God saith." The want of this, is the cause why we have so many distractions and disquiets, and why we are still in our doubtings; even because he that teacheth, and can persuade us, is a deluder.

And hereof it is, that the poor soul saith: " what, shall I have an interest in Christ ? shall I have a title to the promises ? Nay, this belongs to those that are broken-hearted. Indeed if I had such power against corruption, such heavenly-mindedness, and this and that precious grace, there were some hope ; but I am so full of weakness, and many times led captive by such a rebellious heart, that it is too apparent I never had saving grace : nay, I fear I never shall have it truly wrought in my soul."

This you say, poor soul : but who told you so ? and where learned you that religion ? I am sure you never learned it of Christ. For who, or what word tells you, "if I have such a load of corruptions, I shall never have grace ?" Not the word of Christ, I am sure. Wherefore I charge you hold to the truth of the word. Learn of me, saith Christ, and put not your case to be decided by carnal reason ; neither regard what it telleth you. For if you take that way, and turn not back, you can never come to Christ; no way to him that way. Learn of the Lord Christ, for his word is faithful, and his promise sure, and there you shall find a tower of rest as strong as mount Sion. It is that word whereby we shall be judged at the last great day, when sense and feeling shall be cast over the bar for deceivers, and never come into court again.

And thus much of the four cures.   It rests that I now propound four rules, by which a man may know how to order himself, and so to walk, that he may keep a strait course by the word, and not turn aside to the one hand, or to the other, from that guide of his way.   And thus walking, he may get into his hands the evidences that can assure him of a rest perpetual, and establish his mind with perfect peace.   For they work none iniquity, that walk in this way.

CHAPTER III

Rules to direct a Christian how to use the word of God for his evidence, or assurance with peace

T HE first of these rules teacheth to use the word of God aright. For as thou must in all things that concern thy soul repair to the word ; so thou must consider thine own uprightness by it, and see what work is in thy soul that is able to answer the word, and to testify that the work of grace is there. And here be sure to take thy soul at the best. Do not always pore upon the worst that is in it, nor upon thy failings, nor that which can only accuse thee ; but if there be any thing there that may justly speak for thee, neglect not that. It is an injustice for any court to hear one side and not another. The Scripture is a text of justice, and the Lord doth not lie at catch with his children, but takes them at the best: as Rom. 4, 22, it is therefore said that *Abraham believed the promise, and it was imputed to him for righteousness.* Indeed, as in Gen. 12, he had some doubtings ; but God took him at the best: and speaks this of his faith. So Sarah is spoken of as a gracious woman, and a pattern for women, by calling her husband lord ; which was a sign of reverence to her husband, and an humble heart to the Lord.   And yet we read that she derided the message of the Lord by the angel, Gen. 18, 12.   The Lord buries that, and only speaks of that which was to her commendation, and so took her at her best too.   Now as the Lord dealt with these, so should we with ourselves.   Whatsoever is found sincere and upright in us, that should we observe, as well as that which is not so; nay, that rather and before the other.   If a man should have his cause handled in any court of justice after this fashion; namely, that there should only be observed what is failing in the cause, and never that which makes for it; the best cause that is might go to the ground. Therefore the court will hear all read : every bond or bill that shall come in, and every matter of agreement; briefly, every thing.   The cry will be, let all be read.   Again, suppose a man have a bond or other instrument in court, and that the lawyer only doth open and read the failings in it, and that which seems to make against the party. If the judge only hear that, how can it but go against that side?   Therefore that party saith, "good my Lord, hear all."   Now when all is read, those defects are corrected, and the cause goes well, which had not been so, if that bond or deed, or other instrument had been read to halves, not thoroughly.   So when men shall bring in so

many and main indictments against themselves,
and say, " oh what pride and stubbornness is in
my heart! Oh! how weak am I, and dull, and
dead, and backward to holy duties; oh! how
careless of enjoying communion with God! How
negligent in sifting and trying my own heart, in
watching over my senses, and mourning in secret
for my daily failings!" Though this were so, yet
if men will see no more, and these too much, no
marvel if they trouble their own house, or if
Satan by their own words judge them. To such
an one therefore I say, " all that thou sayest may
be true, but art thou not troubled with these failings? And are they not the greatest grief that
thy soul hath?" " Yes," saith the poor soul,
" I confess my heart is vexed, and my soul
grieved for them; and I could be content to be
any thing that I could not be so." Now hear on
this side, and take the best. For as it is with a
man's hand and the staff, so it is here. I compare the promise to a staff; you know the back
of a man's hand cannot take hold of the staff; but
the palm of his hand can. So turn thou the right
side of thy soul to the promise, and then thou
mayest take by it. We take not by it, because
we turn the back side of our hearts to the promise: for then, the soul saith, " oh! my stubbornness is great, and mine inabilities grievous, and
corruptions many." But this is the wrong side;

which will ever hinder thee from taking hold of
the promise.   But turn to the right side, and then
say, " my soul hates these, and my soul is right-
weary of them."   Oh this is the right side ; turn
to that, and thou art well.

Labour to have thy conscience settled and established in that truth, which now out of the word
thou hast gotten to bear witness of the work of
grace in thee.   For if there be any want of the
assurance of God's love, and if the evidence of
the work of grace come not roundly in, but there
be some guilt of sin still remaining ; conscience
will make new stirs and breed new broils, and
continually move and unquiet* the heart.   Therefore as it is good to have our judgment informed
by the word, when we see the good that is in us ;
so it is meet we should make conscience persuaded of it, so as conscience may speak for us, and
all be made strait.   Otherwise, as the debtor that
is indebted to many creditors, if he agree not with
all, or with all save one, that one may come upon
him as well as all the rest ; so for the poor distressed soul that lies at the mercy of the Lord,
and is so deep in arrearages to the law, that he
cannot wind out ; if he labour not to still conscience, and what is else against him, in every
point as well as in some ; if he leave one undis-

* Disquiet.   Ed.

charged, that one may set his conscience against him, as well as an hundred.

The want of this, is the cause why new suits and new bills are daily put in against us; only because conscience is not pacified, nor all quieted. And now take a poor sinner that hath all his doubts and objections answered; come to him, and say, " are all these all your doubts and objections ?" He will say, " yea." " And are they all answered ?" Here he will say " yea, too." " And have you now any thing to say against that which hath been made known unto you ?" " No not now." But say to him again, " did your conscience say to you, it is a sin to say you have no grace ?" Here he demurs and stops, and says, " no, I dare not say so, but I rather say the contrary." And now mark what he says : " all the books are crossed, and all objections answered, and yet conscience puts in a new plea, because haply it was not satisfied to the full, and in every parcel of aberration."

And now come to him again, and say, " you are sometimes captivated by sin, are you not ?" And are you willing to be at God's free disposal, and that he should pluck away all your corruptions, as it were shackles from you ?

" Oh !" saith the poor sinner, " I must needs yield to that." Then I affirm to thy soul, that this is a work of true grace: Here therefore let

conscience be fully satisfied. "But how satisfied?" Thus: cancel all self-accusations, and
this will quit all scores, and clear the heart, scat-
tering all clouds that mist it. This will cast out
all cavils, and all new bills against us: *for if our
consciences condemn us not, then we have boldness
towards God.* We must then stop the mouth of
conscience; that is, be convinced, and agree, that
it is a sin to say, God hath not wrought this work
of grace in the heart, when it is so clear he hath.
For though sense and feeling be, as it sometims will
be, gone, yet conscience remembers the day and
year when the sinner had a clear evidence of
God's love, and therefore saith, "Lord thou
knowest it, and thou didst say out of thy word at
such a time, that the heart of this poor soul was
upright and sincere before thee."

And here it should be with a poor sinner, as
with a wise man, when he would make his lands
sure unto him and his posterity by evidences and
writings sealed. He is not content here only to
have his evidences in his own keeping, but will
have them enrolled in chancery, such a year, and
such a day: that if he should lose his deeds, he
might be sure where to find them. So it should
be with the distressed soul; it should not only be
willing to have all objections to the contrary of it
answered; but it should further get them recorded in the court of conscience, as in chancery;

that when sense and feeling are lost, yet it may readily go to that high court of conscience, and there find the day and year when God's love was made sure unto it.

We should strive, and that mightily to have our hearts overpowered with the evidence that reason and conscience make good unto us; that so we may quietly receive, and calmly welcome it; yea, and yield and subject our hearts to the truth of it. But here we all stick: and there are three things in the soul of a man; three, I say, that abet all these quarrels and oppositions against the evidences of the word in that man. 1. Reason objects. 2. Conscience accuseth. 3. The will of man will not submit. And here we find by experience, that when a man hath stilled conscience, and silenced all reasons to the contrary of his peace; yet such is the iron of the stubborn heart, that nothing can bar it; but still it maintains, and will, some gainsaying and some new quarrels against the truth and itself. Besides, it keeps on foot even that which hath been long ago answered, and let down: nay, that a man would think had been buried in a grave as deep as hell, never to rise again. Now in this case it is with a poor sinner, as with a man that hath a contentious adversary. Haply the cause that they two have in hand, hath been tried in all courts of law, and at last comes to the chancery: and there it is

concluded against the caviling adversary, as in
the other courts.   There all matters are as well
stated and ordered as a man would wish, and as
an honest man would grant.   Yet will not this
man, that is so contentious, be so concluded, or so
yield, but will to the law again with a back suit,
and then, and upon that old grudge, stake down
all he hath, and sell all to his shirt.   His will he
will have, whatever it cost him.   Nor will he
give over, till the judge doth come to take notice
of him, and so to cast out his cause with himself;
whom therefore he commits to prison, and saith,
" sirrah, these matters were all of them long ago
answered, and will you trouble us again, not with
new matters, but with old quarrels ?"

   Just so it is with the heart even of a gracious
man sometimes, and one that is humbled in some
measure ; and could be content to yield to the
commanding power of God's word, and to the
witness of his own conscience: and therefore
saith, my condition is better than I thought it
was ; yet there is an old proud, self-willed heart
still in me ; an heart that will not be quieted nor
said unto ; but still will be quarrelsome, and
maintain the old exception.   For though all reasons
are well confuted, and conscience bears witness it
is so ; and the minister, as the judge under
Christ, cast out the cause: yet observe it, the
poor distressed sinner will keep the old road of

objecting against himself: and though he hath been answered fully, and to every point, not many hours before; yet he keeps old matters still fresh, and out of the salt, till they yield a foul scent to all that come within the hearing of them. And thus, even when a man would think he should not dare to come in court with such old cashiered stuff; yet that proud self-willed heart will be doing still; nor will yield or give over. Have we not just cause then to labour our hearts so far as to get them overpowered with the authority of the truth concerning whatsoever God reveals to them for their good? Oh therefore, poor soul, do not reject the evidence which God makes known, and passeth upon thee for thy sure welfare eternally. Do not, because thou hast not that comfort that thou wouldst, reject all; as if thou wouldst have none at all. So then the fault here is not properly because thou canst not, but because thou wilt not receive the promise. And this is that that so racks and torments thy spirit; this is that which breeds the quarrel so hard to be compounded. And hence it is, that when reason is satisfied, and conscience convinced, yet the soul is perplexed still. For put this question to it, and say unto it, are you persuaded that the Lord hath done you this good, that he will show an everlasting mercy to your soul? And it will say, no; and that all the world shall not persuade it of that. " Ministers are merciful (will such a distempered soul say) and Christians are charitable, and loth to displease too much, or to discourage one in my case, or do to me as I should do to them. But did they know me indeed, they would never think thus of me. Certainly I shall never find it so. What ? Have I grace ? All the world shall never persuade me to it." Mark what I say : this is merely thy pride and self-willedness, that will not receive that good which God is willing to give thee. But repent, or this pride of thy pettish heart will cost thee dear one day ; I wish it may not.

But some will say, " how can you make this pride ? We are ever complaining of, and condemning ourselves ; and can this be pride ?"

Yes, I say, (and mark what I say,) it is intolerable pride against the majesty of heaven. And this I make good by these two things. For,

1. For a man to follow his own conceits and self-willedness against the truth, the force of reason, and the witness of the servants of God, and his own conscience, cannot but be pride.

2. And for a man, because he hath not what he would, to be therefore off the hinges so, as to throw away all God's kindness, and to deny the grace that is given him : and this because he cannot be conqueror as he desires ; is not this pride ? That measure of mercy which God hath already

shown to thy soul, is incomprehensible, beyond
man's reach; and yet because thou canst not
have what thou wouldst, thou wilt have nothing
at all. Just as if a man that hath the law on his
side, and his estate settled on him, should, because his evidences are not written in great golden
letters, nor in the largest royal paper, throw all
away. This is your case : for because you have
not so much of grace, or with such a sweetness
as you would, you deny you have any. But have
you no humility, because none to your mind, or
not so much, or not in such a manner as you require ? Oh pride ; and pride in the highest degree!

These things considered, labour to bring your
hearts more down in a holy subjection to God's
measure and time. And think it your duty, as
well to receive comfort when God offers it upon
good terms, as to do any duty commanded. And
know that it is as truly a sin, though of a higher
size, to reject mercy when God offers it, as to kill a
man, which God hath forbidden. I say, not as
much ; for I know there is difference in the degree.
Therefore you, the saints of God, that have been
thus pestered, and thus possessed to become your
own enemies, remember, when your hearts thus
begin to slide away, to take your hearts unto you,
and not to give them the reins at such desperate
conclusions against God and conscience. Deal

better with your souls, and say, " good Lord, this
is the proud unyielding distemper of this vile
heart of mine. For, what would I have ? Is
not God's word clear in this point, and my conscience satisfied ? Do not the ministers of God
affirm my state to be good ? And shall I thus
dishonour God, and slight them ?"

But what saith the poor soul to this ? " Must I
eat my own words ? Must I say and unsay ?
Say I have grace, when before I said, I had
none ?"

Yes, and be thankful too to God that you may
say so. Is it not better for you to cross your own
flesh, than to cross God's Spirit ? Take notice of
this, and fear lest that proud and peevish soul of
yours, (which now refuseth consolation when
God offers it,) be forced to fare as a man that
eats his own flesh, and so to come upon her knees
for comfort, and get none to her dying day. For
though God will save you at last, yet meanwhile
you shall have an hell upon earth before this be.

One would have thought it had been great humility in Peter to refuse to let Christ wash his
feet ; but it was no such matter. Indeed nothing
less ; therefore Christ takes him up roundly for
it, (which is indeed the only way to cure such a
distemper as this,) John 13, 8, 9. *If I wash thee
not, thou hast no part in me.* If you will needs
have your own way, and humour yourself, and

will not be persuaded, you may go down to hell
in the mind. Peter might have paused here, and
taken breath, but did not. His stout stomach
quickly came down, and he presently said, then,
*Lord, not only my feet, but my hands, and my
head.* It is the humility of a good heart, to take
what God offers. Most Christians think they are
humble-hearted, when yet they are so far proud,
as to give way to this sullen disposition. Therefore labour to master this over-soaring heart of
thine, with the authority of the word of God.
And be sure to receive mercy while God offers it,
lest he draw in, and take away the comfort of his
Spirit from thee, and make thee go howling and
roaring to thy grave. Though he bring thee to
heaven in the end ; yet thou mayest have an uncomfortable hell before thou comest thither.

The last rule is this : maintain the good work
which thy heart hath submitted unto, and keep it
as the best thing in thy house, and of treasure the
best under heaven. And then, when thou hast
by it obtained certain evidence that thy estate is
good; hear nothing against it, but stick fast to it,
as to thy life. Regard nothing which is not in
the word, to the contrary of that evidence of thy
salvation ; that I mean which thou hast been
persuaded of by the word of truth. And here, if
Satan or carnal reason have any thing to say
against thee, let them bring Scripture, and then

yield to it in the true sense; but without the word hear nothing. See how it is with a man that is at law for lands; if he have his adversary on the hip, and have gotten some advantage against him, he will keep him there, and hold him to the point. So do thou in a better case. For if a man will follow every wrangling lawyer at every impertinent quibble or out-leap, he must never look for an end of lawing. And it is the fashion of many attornies, rather to breed quarrels, than to kill them in the conception. So in this case, he that will quarrel where he may resolve, shall never have done. And therefore hold to the main point. Deal with Satan as with a subtle adversary, that is full of wiles and fetches. It is the cunning of the enemy to lead you aside: and he will have many vagaries, if you be in a good way, to bring you out: but be sure to hold to that truth which you have received from the evidence of the word, and the witness of conscience.

How the soul being tempted, may answer Satan's accusations

When a man hath gotten some comfort, then the devil begins to play the lawyer, in this or the like manner.

Satan. Dost thou not see how weak and poor thou art? how destitute of all saving grace, and how contrary thou walkest to God?

It is true, (saith the soul,) yet it is as true, that, *whoso confesseth and forsaketh his sin shall have mercy.* Prov. 28, 13.

But dost thou not see that thou art full of pride and weakness, and secretly unwilling to come to duties?

It is true I am so, yet I hate, and desire to forsake this way, and therefore shall find mercy; the word saith so, Isaiah 55, 7.

But are you of God's counsel? secret things belong to God.

Indeed I know not what God's secret will is; yet that I know, that the word saith, which is, *he hath no pleasure in the death of a sinner,* but invites such daily to come unto him. Ezekiel 33, 11.

But many cozen themselves: mercy is as a black swan, a rare bird; and few obtain it. And why then may not you be cozened as well as others?

But the Lord will not cozen me, and the Lord knows my heart; and the word knows what the Lord knows.

But may not you be deceived in the letter of the word? The word is true indeed; but how know you that you rightly apply it, and that the word and your heart suit together ?

Why I desire as earnestly to have my sin purged, as I do to have it pardoned. I know my heart by the word, and to the word I repair ; and the Lord knows that I hate all sin inwardly, and reform it outwardly, to my weak power ; and therefore I know I shall find mercy. Show me a place of Scripture that saith I do not rightly apply the word, and I believe it ; but I will not believe thee ; for thou art, as thou wast from the beginning, a liar. Thus hold to the word, and the devil will be tired, weary, and leave thee. Keep you here, for if he catch you a wandering after sense and feeling, you are gone. The prophet saith ; Psalm 119, 98. *Thou, through thy commandments, hast made me wiser than my enemies, for they are ever with me.* Satan is wise by long experience ; and the flesh, and carnal reason, and the world are wise too. But blessed be our God that makes every poor ignorant servant of his wiser than all these. But how ? The word must ever be in your hands, and the meditation of it in your hearts. It must be always with you ; and you must keep it with you daily. For that will make you to know not only what is amiss, but to get ground against corruption, and whatever else may hinder your peace with God and with yourselves.

Satan deals in this case with the soul, as the enemies in war. When Joshua defeated the men of Ai, he got them out of the city ; and then they that lay in ambush went and took it, and burnt it with fire. Joshua 8 : 19. So the devil doth. Our castle or city is the promises, the word and ordinances of God : now if the devil can but get you out of this castle, he hath you where he would. If you will look after every bird that flies, and listen after every word of carnal reason and temptation that comes, you are gone. If he can get you from the sure hold of the promise, he will entangle you in his snare of unbelief, and so prevail against you.

Little children, if ye abide in God's command-ments, ye abide in God, saith the apostle. 1 John 2. As if he had said, children, your ene-mies are many, and great, and cunning ; there-fore keep at home, and within the walls of your sure hope, and then you are well, whatsoever weather is up. It is the fashion of parents, if their children run abroad and catch a blow, to tell them that they are well enough served ; you might have kept at home when you had warning. So here.

The issue of the point is this : judge **thy** soul by the word, and look upon that sacred piece in the glass of itself : and here, let it bear witness for thee. And what the word of God doth evidence to thee, that do thou maintain, and hear nothing against it. This is the way to receive constant comfort, and the way to go on cheerfully in thy Christian course. Let quarrels, troubles, and temptations come, yet keep close within doors, and rest thyself upon the riches of that grace that is in Christ Jesus. Then you may be forever comforted, and go singing to heaven, and cheerfully to your graves, though you meet with ever so many temptations and oppositions, crossing your way.

CHAPTER IV

Now follow some means to obtain an interest in
the promises, and improve them for our benefit

It resteth that I show you some means,
whereby a man may so improve his time,
that at last he may obtain this blessed estate of
being glad in the Lord. The means are four.
But before I begin with them, you must know
that we may use the means, and yet find no
means under heaven to do it, except God strike
the stroke. You must therefore wait upon God,
and the Spirit of God in the use of the means for
this matter, by believing rightly to your assurance. For, so the text saith, Phil. 1: 29. *To
you it is given to believe :* it must be given therefore : and *faith is the gift of God*, Eph. 2: 8.
It is God then that must do it ; who yet will not
do it without us, being reasonable men and women
in the power of willing. Again, the Lord affords
us means ; yet not to use them and give Him
the slip. And here it is a good saying ; let the
Lord do what he will, and let us do what we
should. We must not think when we have the
means, that we can get faith presently : for, as
Paul saith, Eph. 1: 20. *The same power that*

*raised up Jesus from the dead, must make us able
to believe;* or else all the angels in heaven, and
all the ministers on earth, and all the help that
men and means can give us, will do us no good.

Now the means are of divers kinds : as, hearing, and prayer, and sacraments, which are the
conduit-pipes through which God communicates
faith. But I let them pass, and fasten upon
those which are needful for feeble Christians, to
the bringing of them into this blessed state of
rightly believing.   And these are such as follow.

1. Means. We must, as much as in us lies,
labour to pull away all those carnal outward
stays that the soul leans upon, and all other like
succours, and whatsoever contentment it is, which
a poor sinner doth betake himself to, as to his
refuge for relief and help ; that when all these
are taken from us, we may be forced to go for
succour thither, where right succour is to be had.
It is a thing natural to us all, even from our first
parents, a desire to have the staff in our own
hands, and to be able to supply ourselves of all
necessaries, without being beholden to others, or
to any.

Now therefore, the way to make the soul to
lean upon Christ, is, to pluck away all those de-
ceiving props.   The last thing we fly unto is the
promise ; which if we could find good any where
else than in Christ, we would never go to him for

it. God hears last of us: and therefore here we should do with ourselves, as the enemy doth with a city besieged, when he would make the inhabitants, or those that keep it, to yield. The way he takes is to famish them, to cut off all provision, and stop all passages, so that none can come to relieve them; then they presently yield themselves to the mercy of the assailant. So it is with our nature. And seeing it is so that we are still trusting to our own strengths, and relying upon something of our own; the best way were to famish the heart, by cutting off all the means and comforts whereby the same is succoured, and quieted, but not rightly in Christ. For when the heart is thus famished, it will then seek out to a Saviour, and there betake itself, because there is no other thing or means otherwise to help it.

The poor woman in the gospel had spent all her goods upon the physicians, Matthew 5: 26, 27, and if she had had but a little means left, yea, but one farthing-token, (for any thing that I know, or doth appear,) she would never have gone to Christ. But when all these failed, then she was forced to seek to Christ, who was ready and willing to do that for her, and more than she desired. Our souls must have something to bear upon, and they cannot subsist without some under-props. Hereupon therefore, when all our carnal hopes are taken from us, we stay, as we must needs, upon the promise, because we have nothing else to rest upon.   Yet it is not required, though I thus speak, that a man should cast away all outward comforts, such as God affords him for the interim here : oh no : but only this ; that though he have much this way, yet that he labour to get his heart to see and acknowledge the insufficiency and nothingness of them all, till he have the superlative comfort, Christ, above all ; and not to repose in them as some do, making them our whole contentment, and sole rest : for then they are but lying vanities, and broken staves, which will not only cozen us, but pierce us too, and that deeply.

And now when the soul seeth that these things cannot succour it, but lay it in a worse case ; a man will then be content to have his heart divorced from them.   And here it is with the soul as it was with Noah's dove, when the ark began to rest upon the mountain of Ararat : Noah then sent out the dove; but the dove found no rest for the sole of her foot.   No question there were many dead carcases to settle upon ; but the dove found no rest, till she came to the ark again.   So when a man finds no rest in any thing the creature affords, and can get no footing for the soul there to stay itself upon ; then he betakes himself to Christ the ark, and goes home to the promise, and rests there, and expects from thence what is needful for him. As therefore in the art of swimming; he that will swim, must pluck his feet from the bottom, and commit himself to the stream to bear him up: so in this our purpose to heaven, we must draw our hearts from these vain things below, and these from them; and though we have honour and preferments, yet we must put no confidence in them, but pluck our affections, as it were feet from them, and learn by our believing to commit ourselves wholly to the power of the promise, and thence to receive comfort, and permanent abiding.

Let not the gods of this world, then, as honour, and profit, and pleasures, deceive thee. Did the pride of Pharaoh's heart deliver him? Did the riches of the rich man in hell save him? Did Herod's applause that he had, do him any good? Did these gods secure them? Nay, have they not left them in the lurch? Therefore let us take our hearts off from these things, and in comparison to those of our better life, have a base esteem of them, and see so great a vanity and emptiness, and insufficiency in them all, that we may be forced to seek to Christ, and say as David, *help Lord, for vain is the help of man.* Labour we further to see the privy wiles of our own hearts, and to hunt out all those mazes, and turnings, and windings of our subtle souls: for here it is wonderful to see how the soul is ready to hang her comforts upon every hedge, and to shift and shirk in every by-corner for them. Now when thou seest thine heart thus seeking comfort in vain helps, call it from them, and pluck them away, and up by the roots, and see the emptiness of them. Then will thy heart be fit and ready to make out to Christ. And this for the first means.

2. Therefore when this is done, there is in some part, some way made for the promise to come into thy soul ; therefore labour thou in the second place, to have thy heart possessed thoroughly, and persuaded effectually of the fulness of that good which is in the promise, and of that satisfactory mercy and freeness of the grace that is in Christ ; so that the soul may be established with that full content which is to be had in the riches of the promise. But mark what I say ; let us persuade our hearts first ; and not content ourselves that we are able to dispute somewhat fully of the excellency of the promise, and of those riches in it, through the free grace of God in Christ. For, what is it to purpose that the heart knows this ; and knowing it, to be so fore-stalled, that it can never come to the promise ? Therefore leave not thy heart till it come to value the promise by that which the word speaketh of it, in a true account. I say, leave not thy heart, till thou see the promise of grace most beautiful in thine eye ; and that thy heart may get some

earnest touching the goodness of God, and the
riches of his grace towards thee by the same.
And here bring thy heart to know and see, that
the promise is better than all the riches and honours that thou canst have, or the world can bestow : for so we read, Psalm 9 : 10. *They that
know thee, will trust in thee ; for thou, Lord,
hast never failed them that seek thee.* If thou
knowest and wilt believe this, this kind of knowledge and persuasion cannot but breed confidence
and resolution, and consequently quiet the heart.
We dare trust a friend whose faithfulness we have
tried ; and we rest upon that which we know by
the sure card of experience. The promises of
God are all of them, as true as gospel. Seek
from one end of the heaven to the other, turn all
the Bible over ; and see if ever any man leaned
on the promise, and the Lord did not perform
what he had promised for the good of his soul.
*Except the Lord had been my delight, I should
have perished in my trouble,* (saith David, Psalm
119 : 92.) *My flesh faileth, and my heart also ;
but thou art the strength of my heart, and my
portion forever.* Psalm 73 : 26.

But here lies a great matter, a work of marvellous difficulty and great necessity ; and therefore, that thy heart may sit down satisfied with
the sufficiency of the promise, I will propound
three rules how the promise may be improved

and conduce to thy singular benefit here and hereafter.

How to improve the Promises for our benefit

For the first of these, labour daily to present thy soul a greater good in the promise, than thou canst see any where else. It is a man's skill, and it should be his endeavour, daily to look narrowly to his heart, and to see what it is that the heart desires most; and accordingly to present the greatest good unto it. And what may that be? Even that which hath more of contentment in it, than any thing else in the world. And here, we should deal with our hearts as men will with a corrupt justice, when they would have him to be on their side; there, the only way is to bribe him. But though it be sinful in that case, yet it is good to bribe, as it were, the corrupt heart with the goodness of the promise; that so the heart may cleave to it, and long after it. Do honours, or riches, or the applause of men, or any earthly pleasures offer thee content and satisfaction? Then persuade thy heart there is a greater worth in the promise, than can be had in all them. For here is an exceeding weight of glory : and he that hath it shall be made a king, and shall have that glory that will never fade. Further, doth thy

heart hanker after earthly joy and mirth? Thou
shalt find more joy in the promise, than in the
cracking of these thorns. Doth thy heart hanker
after riches? Tell thy heart that there are un-
searchable riches in Christ, and that through him
we have a title to all the promises of this life and
a better. We know that he that offers most for
the bargain hath it. Therefore we should observe
the goings-out of our hearts, and what offers are
made to give them the best content, and with
such to present them. This the promise doth;
and this with a greater good in God, than in all
things in the world beside. Therefore, *Oh the
height, and depth, and length, and breadth of
the love of Christ which passeth knowledge!*

The consideration of so much, should not only
work a longing after Christ, and the promise; but
fill our faces with shame and confusion, that ever
we should set so light by sure riches of mercy,
and walk unworthy of so great salvation. Could
we comprehend the unmeasurable dimensions of
God's love and goodness revealed in his word;
O how would our hearts be inflamed towards
him! When the sinner thinks thus with himself;
" I that have done all that I could against so good
a God, that my heart even bleeds to think of it;
there was no name under heaven that I tore in
pieces more, or so much, as God's name; his
wounds, and life, and heart-blood I have rent and

torn a thousand times. Nay, there was no command in the world that my soul so much despised, as the command of the Lord Jesus. There was no spirit which ever spake to me, which I so much resisted as the Spirit of the Almighty. Oh how many sweet emotions hath the Lord let into my soul, thereby to force me from my courses so base, and practices so sinful? By how many mercies hath he allured me ; by how many gracious promises hath he invited me; by how much of his goodness provoked me to forsake my sins, and to turn to him ? But I have flown in the face of his ministers, and blessed Spirit, and rejected all terms of reconciliation. If I had lain in a dungeon, and been plagued with torments all my lifetime ; yea, though I could have had another world full of miseries to live in ; I should count it infinite mercy, so the Lord would pass by my sinful miscarriages, and pardon these inward insurrections.

But that God should send his dearest Son to love me, and that so incomparably, and so unconceivably as that I could not possibly hate him so much, as he loved and affected me ; that I could not so exceed in unkindness towards him, as he hath exceeded in tender kindness towards me ; what a love is this ? What unkindness for so great love ? Were it not righteous with God, never to speak comfort more to my soul, that have so lightly esteemed his promise, and sweet word of comfort? Had it not been just with him now to take all this, as he well might, for an advantage against me? Was it not just that I, who have lived in sin, should have perished in my sins? and as just that I who have so much loved corruption, should have reaped the bitter fruit of it, long ere this? But that the Lord should find an enemy, and not slay him; nay, that he should give his beloved Son out of his own bosom to save him, is a love not to be expressed. O the height of this mercy, beyond all desire or thought! Oh the breadth of this mercy, a breadth without any bounds! Oh the length of this mercy, a length beyond all times! Oh the depth of this mercy, a profundity beyond all expression!

Labour here, therefore, to have access to the promise, and to bring thy soul unto it. Here speak a good word for it, and say, stand off profits, and pleasures, and preferments; room for the Lord Jesus Christ. Thus speak, and set a peerless and most excellent price upon the promise. And be sure of this, for it is a sure rule, whatsoever the soul doth account as best, that it will choose, and leave all others for it. Therefore if the soul could once out-bid the world, and outshoot the devil in his own bow, and put by all those things which the devil casts as rubs in its way of coming to the promise; this labour would be a work of great gain, and usher in the promise itself. For example : when thou seest thy heart look after friends; let those friends usher the way to think on the infinite love and favour of God in Christ, that friend, as he calls himself. And when thy heart would hunt after wealth, let this usher a way to the promise, and say, if the heart find such content in riches, what should it find in the riches of God's grace in Christ ! And thus present a greater good from the promise, than from any thing else ; and thou dealest safely and well for thyself. This for the first rule.

The second rule, labour to bring thy heart to this, that all the things in the world without the promise, are nothing : and that if thou had'st all that the earth can afford, and not the promise, thou hast gotten but the wind, or that which will rather be a curse to thee than a blessing. For, *faith is the substance of things hoped for*, Heb. 11: 1. It gives a kind of being and subsistence to all. So that there is no subsistence in honour or riches, if they subsist not by faith ; and without faith they are clogs and snares to us ; no helpers. Except faith give them their denomination, and a blessing therewith, they are poor and empty things. Our prayers, if they want faith in the promise, are prayers of no substance ; words, and nothing else. On the other side, the most broken and chattering prayers of a poor soul, when a poor creature can scarce utter five words with any sense; yet these, how weak soever, mingled with faith, are a very powerful prayer. So all your hearing, and my preaching hangs upon faith; otherwise they are but lost labour, wanting that which gives a kind of being to whatsoever I speak, or you hear. This for the second rule.

The third rule in this second of means, is this: labor to acquaint thy heart with that good which the promise promiseth: and this, before carnal reason comes and possesses thy heart. Remember here that the promise is most sure, and will come when it shall be most seasonable, and best for thee, and when God sees it most fit; for then, we shall most certainly have it. Heb. 4: 16. *Let us therefore come boldly to the throne of grace, that we may receive comfort and mercy in time of need.* Not when we see it fit, but when God sees it fit and profitable. But this it is which carries away many. Sometimes they are a little affected with the excellency of the riches of God's grace in Christ; and seeing what great things the Lord hath done for their souls, they say, O that I were such a one; and O that I might die the death of the righteous! But when it comes so to pass that they have not what presently they expect, then they cast away their hope; and then

the good promise of God being out of request, the
devil presently steps in and wonderfully prevails
with them.   They should say with the prophet,
Hab. 3 : 17.   *When the fig-tree shall not blos-
som, neither shall the fruit be on the vine, when
the labour of the olive shall fail, and yield no
fruit; then will I rejoice in the Lord, and joy in
the God of my salvation.*   But where no blos-
soms are, nor fruits appear, there all joy goes to
the ground.   We do not consider that comfort
from the promise, and from the Lord Jesus, is then
most seasonable, when we have most need, and,
consequently, may receive most good by it : for
then may we be sure to have the promise so to
surprise our hearts, that they shall be possessed
and made happy with the all-sufficiency of God.
But we go not so far.   This for the second rule,
under the second means.

In the third place, look for all the good which
thou needest and canst desire from that sufficiency which is in the promise ; and do not think of
thyself to add any good unto it, but go to it for all
thy good.   For, there are all the cords of mercy
that must draw thee ; and there is that all-sufficiency that can supply thee ; and therefore look
for all from thence.   But think to bring nothing
thither, nothing (I say) that can be of power to
enable thee to a power of believing.

And here, it is a weak plea for a man to say, I

dare not look to the promise, I cannot believe it; for if I could, (and O that I could,) then I might expect some good fruit from it.

Thou shalt never believe upon these terms. For, thou must not first have faith, and then go to the promise, but must first go to the promise for the power of that faith. From the promise thou must receive power to believe. And therefore say with the prophet, Psalm 119: 49. *O Lord remember thy word to thy servant, wherein thou hast caused me to trust.* When men are enlarged in love to a man, and make fair weather of promises unto him; this persuades him to trust unto them, and to rely upon them for good to come; therefore he saith, "I durst never so much as have thought of it, much less expected it, if you had not promised so much." And even so here; the promise of God, made to the soul, makes the soul to rest upon what is promised.

To expect faith without a promise, is as if a man should expect a crop of corn without seed; for the promise is the immortal seed of God's word, whereby the Spirit breeds this faith in the hearts of all that are his. So Christ, John 5: 25. *The hour is coming, and now is, when the dead shall hear the voice of the Son of God, and they that hear it, shall live.* It is spoken of raising of a dead man from the grave of sin. First, there is the voice of Christ to the soul, before there can be

an echo again of that soul to Christ. And so the
power of the promise must first come to the soul,
and we must first hear the voice of God in the
promise, before we can return an echo back again
to the Lord. The Lord must say, come to me,
before the soul can say, I come, Lord. Therefore when thou seest much deadness, and dead
unfitness of heart in thee to the promise, do not
thou then leave, and give off, and say, "thus I
am, and so it is with me," and so an end; but go
to the promise and say, "whatsoever frailties I
find in myself, yet I will look to the Lord, and to
his promise. For if I want faith, the promise
must settle me, and I must not bring faith to the
promise, but receive faith from it to believe; and
therefore I will wait upon God till he please to
work it.

And now in the last place, labour to submit to
the most equal condition of the promise, not
making more conditions there than God hath
made. Now the promise requires no more of a
man, but that he come and lay hold of mercy.
Therefore do thou require no more. There is
enough in the promise to do thee good; therefore
do thou expect all good from it, and be content
there to take of God whatsoever he hath therein
offered to thy faith. *Buy without money*, saith
the prophet: Isaiah 55: 1, 2. This is the condition that God offers mercy upon, buy wine and

milk, that is, grace and salvation; without money, that is, without any sufficiency of your own. If a man should go running up and down to borrow money before he comes to buy, he may famish before he can come. So the Lord is offering Christ's mercy and salvation without our cost, and saying, come, take it without money; and yet we will run up and down to borrow money of our prayers and other duties also, and from our prayer against corruption, we may be starved spiritually before we can buy at that hand. If we go this way to work, we may quickly lose our labour, and ourselves. And therefore make God's commodities no dearer than God himself makes them. Many a poor soul not remembering this, is kept from coming to the promise. For, O! saith one, "if I were able to master my sins and distempers as such a one can do, then I might with boldness believe." But this is to bring money. But art thou not content to have Christ of free cost; so as he may have thee, and rule in thee, and supply what is wanting to thee, and open thy sores, and heal thy corruptions? Then why goest thou not to the promise with an empty heart; that the Lord may supply thee, and master all thy risings, and make thee a clean heart? But that must come afterwards, as the Lord saith, Ezek. 16 : 6 to 10. *When I passed by thee, and saw thee polluted in thine own blood, behold*

*the time was the time of love ; and I spread my
skirt over thee, and covered thy nakedness ; yea,
I sware unto thee, and entered into a covenant
with thee, and thou becamest mine :* (that is, thou
wast content that God should marry thee in all
thy rags ;) *then I washed thee with water, yea, I
thoroughly washed away thy blood from thee, and
anointed thee with oil ; I clothed thee also with
broidered work*, &c. Here we see that Christ
first marrieth the church to himself ; and then
gives grace, and passeth over his estate to his
spouse. And now, were it not a wonderful great
folly, if some great king should make love to a
poor milk-maid, and she should put it off, and refuse the match, till she were a queen ; when if she
will match with the king, she may be sure to be
made a queen presently. But this comes after,
and not before the marriage. So we must not
look for sanctification the first day, nor till we
come to the Lord in our Christian vocation. For
this is all the Lord requires of us, namely, to see
our sins, to be weary of them, to be content that
the Lord Jesus shall reveal unto us what is amiss,
and seal a pardon for it, and take it away ; and
further give us his grace to take down the old
building, and to set up a new one in us after his
image. For then the Lord will bring us to himself, and into the wedding-chamber ; and then

through his great mercy, all our corruption shall fall to the ground.

And when the Lord hath brought thy unfaithful heart to believe ; then labour to husband this grace well, and to improve it for thy best good, and live by it. It is a marvellous great shame to see those that are born to fair means, I mean the poor saints of God that have a right and title to grace and Christ, yet live at such an under-rate. I would have thee live above the world, though thou hast not a coat to cover thee, nor a house to put thy head in ; yet if thou hast faith, thou art a rich man ; therefore husband thy estate well. It is a shame to see some live, and husband not that estate they have. They live as if they had it not, so full of want, so full of care, so full of pride, so weak, and so unable to master their sins. Whereas the fault is not in the power of faith, nor the promise, nor in the Lord ; for God doth not grudge his people of comfort, but would have his people live cheerfully and have strong consolations and mighty assurance of his love. And therefore the text saith, *rejoice in the Lord always, and again I say, rejoice,* Phil. 4 : 4. And so Heb. 6 : 18. *God hath sworn ; that by two immutable things, wherein it is impossible for God to lie, we might have strong consolations.* Nay, the Lord rejoiceth in the prosperity of his servants, and therefore hath richly provided for you, that you may re-

joice.   And in not doing so, we offer a great deal
of wrong to the Lord and his promises, and bring
an ill report upon that grace and mercy of his.
And we hereby also open the mouths of the wicked, and make them say, " Oh, these precise people
talk of quiet and contentment, and joy in the Holy
Ghost !   There is great talking of these things,
but we could never see it yet."   O brethren, it
is a great shame.   Are the riches and revenues of
faith so great, that a Christian may live like a
man all his days ?   Let all the drunkards and ma-
licious wretches against God laugh and be merry ;
yet they cannot see one of those days that a poor
saint can ; yea, though he lay in prison all his life
long, Matthew 17 : 20.   *If a man had but faith
as a grain of mustard-seed, and shall say to this
mountain, go hence, it shall be done.*   Whether
this be spoken of justifying faith, or no, I will not
now dispute ; but this I am sure of, *resist the
devil and he will flee from you*, James 4: 7.   And
you may trample under all your lusts and corruptions.   This is the life of faith ; and this life
we may live, this life we ought to live.   If a
tradesman have a fair stock and quick returns, if
he goes down the wind, and begin to decline and
decay ; every man will say, he was left marvellous well, but either he knew not how to use it,
wanting skill, or else attended not on it, wanting
care ; another man would have lived bravely upon

half of that means which he had. So there is never a poor Christian, which trades in a Christian course, but he hath a fair estate, and may live like a man. One promise is enough to make a man live comfortably all his days, though he were in ever so much want. But if he be cast behind-hand, and goes down the wind with comfort and joy ; and sinks because of his pride, and distempers and vexation : the fault is not in the estate ; for the Lord left him very well. He had a child's portion, had he had an heart to fear God and love him ; as David saith, *Oh be merciful unto me, as thou useth to do unto those that love and fear thy name.* The fault was not in the promises, that they could not, nor in his faith that it would not help him. But he let the promises lie by ; they came into the table, but he never cast them up, nor husbanded them aright. He had a world of consolations, that would have given a man liberty in prison, honour in shame and disgrace, and comfort in time of distress ; but he did not husband them. And therefore be advised to do as the tradesman doth ; he will not spend of his stock, but live of his trading. O I would have every Christian live of his faith. Whatever strength thou needest, fetch it from grace in Christ ; and whatever comfort thou wantest, fetch it from Christ. But live by faith, and make a good living of it too ; and then thou hast improved the promise aright. Bring but an empty believing heart with thee, and the oil will never fail, and the meal in the barrel will never decay, but continually supply thee, as it did that poor widow.

CHAPTER V

*How shall a man be trained up, that he may get
the skill of living by faith*

E VERY man hath his shifts and tricks, and
lives by his own devices; and the devil
hath enough of them in the world that live this
life; but the best life of all is little looked after.

Now for an answer, know thus much, that
there are three particulars for the training up the
heart to learn this skill of living by faith.

1. We must labour to get matter for our faith
to work upon.

2. We must labour to fit faith for the work.

3. We must labour to order our faith aright in
the work.

I. First, we must provide matter for our faith to
work upon. For this we see ordinarily, if a
workman want matter to work upon, either a
carpenter or the like; he must needs cease his
work, and he can go no further. And if a man's
work fails, how can he provide for his family?
This is the complaint of poor people now-a-days,
that they have no work. So it is in a Christian's
course; many poor Christians that are newly set
up, and are not aforehand in the world, they want

even matter for their faith. I mean some are
ignorant and cannot read, and some have not
means of a preaching-ministry, others have but
small parts and cannot hear, and little do they
retain of what they do hear. The promises of God
are not understood, nor remembered, nor rightly
applied. They live marvellously poor, when
they might live very comfortably in the world.

Now the matter of our faith, is the whole word
of God. As the spider gathers poison out of every
flower; so the bee gathers honey out of the same
flowers, and out of the sweetest flower she sucks
the most honey. Oh the word of God, how full
of sweet flowers is it! There, the sharpest terrors, and the most fearful plagues too. A gracious heart will gather sweetness out of both of
these. But above all, the sweet of the promises
of the gospel, the sap and sweet therein, and the
blood of the Lord Jesus Christ that is communica-
ted thereby: oh the faithful soul sucks most
there. Now that we may provide matter for our
faith, observe these rules, which are commonly
observed in all provisions.

First, that they provide and lay in, in season,
timely, as soon as they can. This is the practice
of him that would husband his estate wisely; his
care is to buy at the best hand. So I would have
a good Christian to store up all the promises of
God, in all the good word of God seasonably. I

mean when all thy parts and abilities are strong, and nature is able to fight it out ; and while the fair day of God's favour lasteth ; and while the word and sacraments are dispensed ; this is the best time to lay in spiritual provisions, that we may not want them, when we have use for them. It is a marvellous strange and preposterous course when a man is weak, his eyes dim, and his heart and strength faileth, and even ready to give up the ghost ; then to lay in grace and provision of mercy. And then for him who hath hated the ministers, and loathed the means of grace, and abused the patience and long-suffering of God ; oh then to have a minister come to him, and have a promise in the day of persecution ; then for a man to bethink himself of the promises and comforts of the gospel ; when a man should spend on the promises, then to be getting of them ; this is ill husbandry. The better way is this, to be buying and getting in at every turn. And this is the reason why our Saviour saith, Luke 19 : 42. *O if thou hadst known, in this thy day, the things that belong unto thy peace!* While the word, and thy life, and the Sabbaths, and the ordinances last ; this is thy day ; we know not how soon the Lord may take all from us. Oh the estate of the poor Palatinates ! if it be true we hear of them, they have lost all the means of grace, and they have idolatry now amongst them, and their ene-

mies force them to go to mass against their consciences ; and they cannot see a good minister,
nor a good Christian, but they weep to consider
the times they once had.   Therefore let us labour
to be wise in the Lord, now while the fair is ; and
consider how God deals with his children : Psalm
48 : 9.   *We have thought of thy loving kindness,*
O God, in the midst of thy temple.   It is spoken
there of the goodness of God towards Sion.   She
was a cup of poison, and a stone of stumbling :
when he had spoken of all the bulwarks that God
had made, and all the goodness and mercy he had
shown to his people, and the malice and wrath of
his enemies : he saith, *this God is our God even*
forever and ever, verse 14.   As if he had said,
the Lord did provide for his people in Egypt, and
overthrew proud Pharaoh that set himself against
God ; and this is our God.   When thou art in
the wilderness, this God is thy God ; when thou
art in persecution, this God is thy God, and the
God of all.   Thus he stores up while the season
lasts.

2. Note this, as thou must observe what God
doth to others, so labour to treasure up thy own
experiences, he hath delivered us, and he doth
and will deliver us, saith the apostle : 2 Cor. 1 :
10, and 1 Tim. 4 : 18.   And the prophet David
saith, Psalm 119 : 52.   *I remembered thy judg-*
ments of old.   Oh well fare a good old store : I

remember, saith he, how thou didst rebuke Amalek, and overthrow Nimrod, and Ahithophel. Oh it is admirable to consider these things. I received comfort, saith he. God will overthrow every enemy. And this is store for thy faith to work upon, Psalm 89 : 49. *Where are thy former loving-kindnesses ?* David is aforehand with God now ; he is not come to buy food just at the time of famine, but it is laid up beforehand. Lay in abundantly of all the promises of all kinds ; you had better leave than lack. And it is the wisdom of a man to have somewhat to spare, and to have an overplus aforehand ; that a man may not live feebly and poorly, and be at his wits-end at every turn, and know not which way to shift for himself, and have no bread in his house ; I mean, no provision of promises by him : Isaiah 42 : 23. *Who is wise, let him hear for the time to come :* as if he had said, you must not only lay in promises for the present, but store them for afterwards. As the chapman saith, I shall want this at such a time ; and so the husbandman saith, I shall have occasion for this or that at such a time, and so get it aforehand. Oh that God would give us these hearts ! It is good, as we may say, to keep promises in store, that we may spend them at leisure. *In the days of famine,* saith the prophet, *thou shalt have enough,* Psalm 37 : 19. These precious promises will be good meat in lent; when haply thou shalt sit under a hollow tree, and creep among the bushes, then three or four of these promises will give a man a good meal of comfort; therefore store them up, they will do you no harm. And when you are driven from house and home, and friends, and all, these will exceedingly refresh. Oh how sweetly are they scattered up and down in the word, according to the saints several necessities and occasions. Bring this precious provision home, leave it not in the market; it is a folly to say, I have good provision, but it is not here. *Let the word of God dwell plenteously in you, and richly in all wisdom*, Col. 3: 16. Observe, it must be plenty, not scant; it must dwell in you, that you may but step aside and have it; there is the matter for your faith to work on. So also

II. In the next place, we are to fit faith for the service; that it may succeed with more comfort and better speed. Though a man be a believer, yet there is a great deal of dullness and bluntness comes upon this grace, though he have it. See how our Saviour, chides his disciples, *oh fools, and slow and dull of heart to believe*, &c. So we ought to whet our faith, that it may line and square the promises, (as it is in the Hebrew,) that it may pierce through the veil of all the riches of the freeness of God's grace, and so bring comfort to us. It is with the hand of faith, as it is with the hand of the body ; if it be numbed, stiff, or frozen, a man must rub it, or warm it, before he can hold any thing. So it is with the hand of faith, for faith is the hand of the soul, it takes hold of that mercy which God hath provided for us in Christ Jesus. Now faith is sometimes benumbed and stiff through carelessness and looseness. Therefore it is not enough for a man to have faith, but he must supple and oil the sinews of faith, that he may more freely take hold of the promises of life, and receive comfort from thence. And that this may be done, we must,

1. Maintain the evidence of faith once gotten. With question undeniable, this grace of faith once gotten, is to be maintained. Mark it, I speak not of those who have not faith ; it is in vain to bid a man live by faith, who hath none : but it is for those in whose hearts God hath been pleased to work this blessed grace. This must be the care of those that have gotten faith ; they must know the nature of faith in general, and of this faith in particular, whether it be of that faith which Peter speaks of ; for there is a great deal of copperfaith* in the world. As, that Jesus Christ came into the world to save sinners, and the like. Now when thou hast gained evidence that thou hast faith, then fill it up, and keep it by thee, and

* Counterfeit. Ed.

labour to make the demonstration of it so plain to thy soul, that it may be undeniable. What a great folly is it for a man to question, when he should use it? The work must needs be much hindered, though he have never so much faith, when he begins to cavil with it, and to question whether it be good or no. It is a proverbial speech; he that doubts of his way, misseth his way; for while he is doubting, he goes no way in conclusion. So he that questions whether he hath faith, or no, gets little good at present by it. Tell a poor sinner of living by faith, and he says, it is good news if he had it. It is poor comfort to bid a man go warm him when he hath no fire; so it is poor comfort to bid a man live by that which he never had. Quarrelling and doubting when a man hath it, hinders the use and benefit of faith: here is a man that is quarrelling about it, when he should live on it. Matthew 14 : 22—31. When the disciples saw Jesus walking on the sea, they thought it was a Spirit; but Jesus said unto them, *be of good comfort, it is I.* Now when Peter knew it was Christ, being somewhat too venturous, he said, *if it be thou, Lord, bid me come unto thee on the water.* Christ said, come. Peter going, the water began to be boisterous, his heart began to sink, and Christ said unto him, *O thou of little faith, why dost thou doubt?* As if he had said, it is now no time of doubting, but a time of believing. The Lord bid him come, and he had ground enough to come, and strength of faith to come; but when he saw the waves great and troublesome, instead of believing, he fell a questioning and quarrelling with the promise. As it is with a foul rusty musket; shoot such a one off, and it will recoil. When faith grows rusty with doubting, we sit down dismayed and unsettled. The very questioning and quarrelling against the work of faith, many times doth as much disable a man to put forth the power of faith, as if he had no faith at all.

2. When thou hast maintained the clearness of the work of grace before gained, then labour to bring thy heart to marvellous stillness and calmness from time to time. Staidness and stillness of the soul, frame the heart to hold the shield steadily, and bear off the blow comfortably when it comes. Those boisterous affections, those crowds and troops of troublesome imaginations, as fear and jealousy; these unrank* the frame of the soul, that it is not at the command of faith. As it is in an army, when ranks and files are broken, they are at a rout; be the commander never so skillful, he cannot in that condition march on: so though we had never so vigourous a faith, yet if the soul were hurled up and down

---

* Discompose. Ed.

with those boisterous distempers, the soul could
not command faith.   When it was told the disciples, Luke 24: 41, that Christ was risen from
the dead, and had manifested himself to them ;
the text saith, *they believed not for joy and won-
dered.*   They would not believe for a while; and
it was through the violence of their joy, which
gave them no leisure to believe.   As it is true of
moderate affection, so it is true of strong fear, and
cares and distempers ; because these hurry the
soul violently, and transport it so, the man cannot
believe.   As it is in a road, the traveller is fitted
to go his journey, but he is hindered because the
crowd is so great and strong, that they cross him,
and oppose him, and are ready to carry him another
way against his will ; just so it is with a soul thus
troubled with tumultuous thoughts, especially
melancholy, and those other enemies of the soul,
vain imaginations, sinful fears, sinful sorrow, distempered thoughts and cares.   Though the heart
is willing and able to believe, yet those stirrings
of boisterous affections, cross faith in the way,
and bear it down.   There David chides his heart
in Psalm 42 : 5, 11, and 43 : 5, even rocks it
asleep, and would bring it quiet, saying, *why art
thou so disquieted, O my soul, why art thou disquieted within me?* &c.   There are three things
fit our purpose in this text.

1. That a tumultuous distemper of heart makes

a man lie flat upon his back, as it were, and sink into a swoon.

2. It hinders the work of faith. Mark what follows : *hope thou in God.* As if he had said, leave those distempers of heart, and rest upon the freeness of God's grace.

3. David yet looks up to God for mercy : *for he is yet my God.* The virtue of this rule we find by experience ; especially in melancholy persons, when they have swarms of thoughts buzzing in their minds. Sometimes restless fears do chase their hearts, as the hound does the deer in the forest. And after this comes another affection, and after that another ; and so at last they come all together. Sometimes the horror of a man's conscience makes hue and cry after him, and makes him say, " oh how my heart smites me ! Methought I saw hell gaping for me, and the devil even standing at my elbow, ready to carry me down to everlasting destruction :" This makes his soul to have such an amazement and ghastliness of spirit, that he cannot reach the promise of God. Well, take the Lord's advice by the prophet : Exodus 14 : 13. *Fear not, but stand still, and see the salvation of the Lord.* Lay aside those restless imaginations, and those crowds of foolish conceits ; stand still, and be quiet, and with the eye of faith behold the salvation of God.

A third rule how faith may be fitted for the work : take notice of this ; in the want of any means, do not first seek for them ; and in the presence of any means God affords, look not first to them for succour and supply, but first go to the promise, that it may supply what you need, and that the promise may bless what means you have. It is an uncomfortable and disorderly course, for a man barely and first to look at those things which are within the compass of sense, and so range up and down in the use of the means ; when the promise and Christ are the last thought of in our hearts. As for instance. In a time of poverty, how doth the soul unfit itself for the promise? When a man sees his estate low, and he is like to come to misery, he saith, " I have some good friends that will not see me want, I have so much means left yet, and I have my health and strength, and I hope to get a poor living." Not one word all this while of a promise. But what say you to this ? If death take away all thy friends, sickness take away thy health and strength, fire or thieves take away all thy goods, whither wilt thou now go ? Why then at a dead lift, as we commonly say, he is fain to go to that mercy which endureth forever. Oh friend, are you there now ? Why came you not thither at first ? Well, since thou art come, reason thus : " I am like to be poor, and my friends may die, and thieves may rob me of all my goods, but *the mercy of the Lord endureth forever*." So a minister that is faithful, desires to preach fruitfully, and to the benefit of the congregation; and then we catch at the helps that are near at hand, and we go to our books and studies, our wits and pains, and think these will do the deed. We do well in all this; but the fault is in the order of doing them. Haply God knocks off man's wheels, and a man is not able to come to the bottom of the point; and if he be able to compass the truth in some measure, yet God blasts all he doth, and there is no good comes to the souls of his people. At last he is fain to go to the promise; and then the poor minister saith, "Lord, thou hast said thou wilt be with thy faithful ministers to the end of the world; little strength there is in us; but be thou with us Lord:" now the work goes on again. The tradesman is honest and painstaking, and he hopes to compass a good estate by his calling. His stock is good and great, and his skill is sufficient, and his pennyworth shall be as reasonable as any others, and his acquaintance are many. Then God blasts all these, and then he comes to the promise, as in Psalm 1: 3. *Whatsoever the righteous doth, it shall prosper.* Hold here now, and say, "I expect all from the promise, mercy and succour from the promise." This was the course that Jacob took, Gen. 32:

9, first he wrestled with God and overcame him ; then he wrestled with his brother Esau, and saith, *O God of my father Abraham, and God of my father Isaac, which saidst unto me, return into thine own country, and I will do thee good ; I am not worthy the least of all thy mercies : Lord deliver me from the hand of my brother Esau, for I fear him.* Thus he wrestled with the Lord, by virtue of a promise, overcame him, and then overcame his brother Esau. So Hebrews 13 : 5. *Let your conversation be without covetousness ; and be content with such things as ye have.* But how will you have help against this covetousness ? A man would have said thus ; " you have a good portion, and but little charge, and many friends :" But God takes such a course as this ; he saith, *I will never leave thee nor forsake thee.* And thus when I have chased away doubting, then faith is ready, and the shield is scoured.

III. Now for the ordering of faith in the work ; there are two things to be attended to.

1. How the soul should get to the promises.

2. How the soul should take, receive, and improve this sufficiency and excellency that is in God, through Christ and the promise.

1. How the soul should get to the promise : you see all is ready, the way open, and faith is fitted ; there are three rules to be observed, how the soul may get to the promise.

1. Throw off all power and ability in thyself. *Nevertheless*, saith the apostle, *I live; yet not I, but Christ liveth in me*, Gal. 2: 20. It is not I that live by any power of myself, but Christ liveth in me. It was Christ's quickening, reviving, and enabling, though he had faith. *I know*, saith the prophet, Jer. 10: 23, *that the way of man is not in himself, neither is it in man to direct his own steps.* So do thou say, if ever thou wouldst have thy heart fitted to go to the promise; "it is not here, Lord, it is not in this vain mind, it is not in the power of this dead heart, or any passage that ever I received, whereby I am able to believe in thee." I mean the principle of life is not here, the root of faith is in the promise, and from thence it comes into the soul. As it is with a mariner, when the ship is upon the ground in the ebb and low water, he doth not expect to tug his ship to the shore by any power of himself. So, "it is not in my wisdom that can direct me, and it is not in my weapon that can defend; it is not this humility that can bring my soul down; it is not here, it is not I, Lord, that can rest, or go to a promise; even all our abilities are at a low ebb." All that we are, or can do, is to empty ourselves, and fit ourselves, and get up the mainsail; that is, let the soul be ready for a promise, and by virtue of that be carried heaven-ward and Christ-ward. Take notice of this in your own souls, that the

heart would begin at home. If a temptation
come, the heart of itself would overcome it; and
if a duty be to be done, the heart of itself would
perform it; and if opposition come, the heart of
itself would resist it. O remember that a man
offers an injury against reason, sense, and religion,
and all. Now thy faith begins to wrestle with
him and his dealing; and conscience checks, and
thou wilt tear thy own heart out of thine own
bosom. Brethren, this will not do it: when a
ship of an hundred tons is upon the ground, the
mariners may pull and tug their hearts out, ere
they make her go. Oh go then and say, " it is
not I that can be patient, and put up a wrong."
Be quiet, expect it not from hence. Let the
heart lie still, till the wind and tide, and promise
come, and that will carry thee.

Bring the promise home to thy heart, that the
promise may bring thy heart to it. And thus I
would have you reason: the Lord Jesus Christ,
by the power of his Spirit, is in the promise unde-
niably, and undoubtedly, and unspeakably accompanying in his manner, as he shall see fit. This I
say, that the almighty power of Christ doth really
and continually accompany the promise for the
good of his. Hence it is called, the Spirit of
promise; for there is an almighty creating work
goes along with the promise. And I reason thus,
that word which discerns the thoughts of the

hearts of men, that word must needs have the almighty work of God's Spirit accompanying it. So far as God hath promised it, not when t hou haply thinkest it fit, but when God sees it fit. He doth it as a voluntary workman ; therefore thou considerest that there is an almighty power, and a fullness in the promise. Then lay that promise upon thy own heart, and conclude it, and look for virtue from thence, to draw thy soul to it again.

I have several passages to express this more fully. Jacob would not believe that Joseph was alive ; or if he were alive, he had but little means, and was poor, Gen. 45 : 26—29. *But when he saw the chariots that Joseph had sent him, then he believed, and said, 1 have enough ; Joseph my son liveth.* The chariots sent from Joseph to Jacob, brought Jacob to Joseph. So every believing soul is poor and feeble, and disabled to go to God, and to believe in the Lord Jesus Christ. Therefore look thou unto the chariots of Israel first, and that will convey thee to the promise. As it is with the miller, first he prepares the mill fitly, and orders all the occasions thereof ; and when the stones are fit, and laid to go, yet it will not, till the sluice be pulled up, and the water run that drives the mill. So the soul is humbled, and lies level with the Lord and his truth, and is content to yield to his con-

ditions ; but now the soul of itself, in itself cannot
go, it hath not the principle of going ; but let
down the sluice of the promise, and let that come
to thy heart, and it will bring thy soul home to
the Lord.   As Luke 19 : 9.   *This day is salvation come to this house :* not to the walls of thy
house, but to men that are in thy house.   They
did not come to salvation, but salvation came to
them.   The Lord sent salvation to salute the
house of little Zaccheus.

When the promise is thus come home to thee,
and thou seest the sufficiency and authority of it,
then all thou hast to do is this ; in the stream of
that promise, be carried home to the promise.
The prodigal, Luke 15, is said to be like a lost
sheep.   (Mark this, for it concerns you, poor
creatures.)   The poor sheep is wandering up and
down, now in the mouth of the lion, and then in
the briars, and sometimes in the pit.   The text
saith, *he leaveth ninety-nine to seek that.*   That
is, in comparison of what care he expresseth to
the lost sheep ; he leaveth a man regenerate not
carelessly, but he will not express so great love
as to a poor lost man.   And though thou canst
not find the way to heaven, yet he will find it for
thee ; rest thou upon Jesus Christ.   When thou
findest thy heart feeble and weak, and thyself unable to believe ; then the Lord Jesus Christ brings
the Spirit of grace, and that come to seek, and

Jesus Christ lays that soul of thine upon his shoulders, that is, upon the riches of the freeness of his grace. Therefore let thy heart be transported by the power of that grace, and by the virtue of that mercy which God hath made known to thee for thy everlasting good. When the chariots are come, get up into them. The Lord Jesus Christ is gone up to heaven, and hath sent these chariots for thee; therefore get thee up, and say, "Lord, take me up with thee." When the mariner hath sea-room enough, he cares for no man; he looks not so much at his oar, or any thing, so that he can but observe the channel. This channel is but the full tide of promise; therefore lay thyself upon the promise, and say, "Lord, in the virtue of that grace, and in the power of that spirit, carry me; and in the riches of that mercy of thine, Lord convey the heart of this poor sinner, and make me happy with thyself forever."

Again, never let a quick stock lie dead by you; it is monstrous* ill husbandry not to be trading with a quick stock. As it is in the world with temporals, even so it is in our spiritual estate. Though a man have a little for the present, yet if he have some old reversions to come, it will refresh his heart, and bear him up in time of poverty

---

* Exceeding. Ed.

and misery; and he saith, if he can make but a shift for a while, for so long time, then he hopes to live as well as any man in the country. So there are some of the promises we have in possession. Oh, but there is the reversion of old promises, old rents. As old rents of farms that were let long ago, when the leases come out, they are worth treble the rent they were let for at the first: so there are old rents of comfort and mercy; as, *come ye blessed of my Father, inherit the kingdom prepared for you.* Then no more tears, no more trouble, no more sorrow, no more sin. Oh get those into your hands, and have them in use, and say, " the day will come when we shall have happiness and joy beyond all that the tongue of man can express, or the heart conceive. Though we are buffeted with many temptations, and wearied with a world of corruptions, yet we shall be saved," saith faith. Thus a man may make a pretty good shift to live upon these terms, though we have nothing else to live upon in the world. Remember what I speak now, and labour to fasten this truth upon thy heart; that there is not only present good in thyself, but in another, and reserved by another for thy comfort, and be thou content it should be so. Not only to look and see what thou hast, but consider that the greatest part of thy glory, is in the glory of Christ; and the greatest part of thy wisdom, is in the wisdom

of Christ ; and the greatest part of thy liberty, is
in the liberty of Christ ; and thy riches, in the
riches of Christ. And know, whatever is in
Christ thou hast it all as thine, 1 John 3 : 1, 2.
*Behold what manner of love the Father hath be-
stowed upon us, that we are now the sons of God!*
I tell you brethren, this is a marvellous privilege ;
and if you had no more but this, you had a child's
portion. But it appears not what we shall have,
we have but a glimpse now ; what think you will
the harvest be ? Now we have but the sips of it,
what shall then the full cups be when we shall
see Christ as he is ? Thus did Moses improve
his estate, Heb. 11 : 26. He bore all afflictions
comfortably ; yea, *he esteemed the reproach of
Christ greater riches than the treasures of Egypt ;*
why ? *because he had an eye to the recompense of
reward.* We account not of a man's estate for
what he hath in present possession ; but what is
likely to befall him, and what he is born unto.
What Moses did, do thou : remember thou hast a
good stock upon the ground, which will pay all
thy debt, and yet live like a man too. Though
thou hast many corruptions, many disgraces cast
upon thee ; though thou hast little strength, and
art at a great loss in point of comfort ; yet there is
enough in heaven, enough in Christ, both of
riches and comfort. Let thy soul then be careful

to make all these present with thee for thine own good.

But some will ask, how may a man expect that from the promise, which God intends, and will undoubtedly bestow ?

For answer hereunto, I will show what thou mayest expect, and what God will undoubtedly bestow. If thou dost believe, heaven and salvation are certainly thine, and perseverance to the end, and that manner and measure of assistance, that may make thee fit for perseverance : these three things grow here. But for temporal blessings which we desire, and that measure of spiritual blessings which we would have ; so much grace, and so much assistance, and so much abilities to do duties ; God doth not engage himself to bestow these. But that which God engageth himself to bestow, both for temporal and spiritual blessings,—it may be discovered in these three particulars : so much grace and assurance of God's love, and so much comfort in grace as he sees fit for thee, after his own order, and in his own time. I will open them all, because many do here bungle wonderfully.

1. He will bestow them in his own order, not thy order. First, he will make thee fit, and make thee good, that thou mayest be able to digest them, and then he will bestow them on

thee. Haply a poor. man is driven to desperate
hazard, and is brought miserably under, and therefore the heart cries earnestly for some more supply.
He calls and God answers not. And he labours
to look up to the promise, where God saith,
nothing shall be wanting to him, and yet it cometh not. I say, God will give these in his own
order. First, God will make thee fit for this
estate, and then give it. I never knew a good
man desperately poor, but his heart was desperately proud ; therefore the Lord will make him
good, and make his proud heart yield, and then
bestow these things : look for that first, and then
for the other.

Again, another Christian labours exceedingly
for the assurance of God's love, and cannot obtain
it ; and seeks to God in the use of the promises,
and yet he cannot find it settled. Well, God will
give thee comfort and consolation, but in his own
order. And know this, that commonly the Lord
never debars the soul of comfort, but he sees the
heart is not fit for it. Thy heart would be proud
and careless, and God would hear no more of thee,
and thy sail would overturn the boat. Therefore
when God has abased thy heart, and made thee
content to want what he shall deny, then he will
give thee assurance, but it must be in his own
order. And this is the reason why the most
smoke out their days in discontent ; the reason is,

there is a proud heart and a sturdy disposition of spirit that will not come unto God's terms.   As it is with a physician ; he will not give a cordial to his patient, when he will.   For if he were in a burning fever, it were the next way to send him going.   But first he purges him, and makes him fit, and then gives him a cordial.   So it is in these things which thou cravest ; the Lord will give thee them, when thou shalt not surfeit of comfort, and assurance, and prosperity ; and when thy heart is emptied and purged, and able to digest these things, then the Lord will give them.

2. The Lord will give us temporal blessings, and that measure of spiritual, in his own due time ; not when thou and I would, but when he sees most fit ; as John 2 : 3, 4.   The mother of Jesus comes to our Saviour, and saith, *they have no wine.*   She thought she had Christ at command : but he answers her, *woman, what have I to do with thee ? mine hour is not yet come.*   So it is with our souls ; we want comfort, and we want strength against our corruptions, and we want assurance, and assistance : but what have I to do with that proud heart, says our Saviour ?   My time is not yet come.   You would have it now, as they said, Acts 1 : 6.   *Lord, wilt thou now restore the kingdom to Israel ?*   God will do in his own time, and we must wait his leisure.   This is one thing that doth necessarily accompany the

covenant of grace, as I have showed before that
the Lord would dispense the blessings of his kingdom when he pleaseth, and not when we will.
When the Lord sees these blessings of spiritual
mercies and temporal favours are ripe and most
seasonable to thy necessity ; then thou shalt have
them : but the time is in God's hand.

3. The Lord doth not promise in such a manner and measure, and such a peculiar thing, to
give that temporal blessing, and that spiritual
assistance we desire. But the Lord will do that
which he knows most fit. For so the text says,
Prov. 30 : 8. *Feed me with food convenient for
me.* There was faith now ; he wholly refers
himself to God. When a man comes to the tailor
to have a garment made, he doth not cut out the
garment himself, but refers it to the judgment of
the workman. So must we do, refer ourselves to
God ; and know, God promiseth nothing, but as
he sees it fit for thy good. It may be thou shalt
not have this blessing, or that grace. As it is
with a potter, he is minded to make so many ves-
sels of honour : so if the Lord will make thee a
vessel of honour, go away contented; whether
thou hast so much prosperity, and so much good,
or no, and so much grace it matters not so much ;
it is enough that thou art elected to eternal happiness.

Now you see how to manage and improve the

promise aright for your best advantage, and to
expect that from the promise which it will yield.

Another particular in this third rule of living
by faith, is this ; how to take, and how to enjoy
the sap and sweet of the promise, and to live by
it. When the husbandman hath sown his ground,
and his fruit is ripe, and he hath reaped it, then
he must gather in his corn that he may live upon
it. So let us gather in the promises when we see
the best advantage. Now let us take the gain,
and live by it, and that comfortably too, in the
proof of God's goodness therein. For this end,
let me suggest these five directions.

1. Thou seest what God is in the promise, and
thou expectest no more than God is there. Then,
eye that particular good in the promise which
thou standest in need of ; eye that good in Christ
and in the promise, and then set God's power
and faithfulness a-work to bring that good, and his
wisdom to continue it. As for instance : I am in
persecution, and either I would have deliverance
and safety, that I might not be imprisoned ; or
else comfort and refreshment, if the Lord carry
me thither ; and therefore I would see all this in
the promise, still reserving the conditions before-
mentioned. If thou art in prison, eye liberty and
preservation in Christ ; he that is the great de-
liverer of his people, and carrieth his people in his
own hands : and then set God's power and faith-

fulness a-work, that can do it;* and his wisdom, that can continue it for thy good. That which thou seest and needest in the promise, that the power and wisdom of God may communicate to thy soul. This is the meaning of that place, Psalm 37: 5. *Commit thy ways unto the Lord, trust in him, and he shall bring it to pass.* Roll thyself, and lay all thy occasions upon the Lord. Therefore the apostle saith, 1 Peter 5 : 7. *Cast your care upon the Lord, for he careth for you.* It is God's proper office and work : he careth for thy soul, therefore lay it all upon him, and put over all thy care into his hands, and set his power and faithfulness to do the work : only this is here a little to be scanned. I speak not this, that we should take no care at all, but I say, hang all the weight and burden upon the Lord. The brewer, he tumbles the barrel of beer, and he rolls it, but it is the earth that bears it. So whatever trouble is in thine eye, or ear, or heart, roll it upon the Lord. That is, the weight of a man lies especially in three things, which a man must hurl off himself and lay upon the Lord. Either first, a man shall not be able to know what he shall do,

* The design of the author, in this rather peculiar expression, used here and elsewhere, doubtless was, to recommend the believer's humble and prayerful endeavors to engage the divine power for his aid, in circumstances of spiritual extremity. ED.

or what he is commanded. Or else, secondly, he shall not be able to do what God commands, and he knows. Or else, thirdly, he shall not find success in what he doth. It is not a trouble to do what we can, or to employ ourselves as we are able. But this is the trouble when the heart saith, " I know not what the mind of God is ; or, I shall not do what I know; or, it will not succeed ; or, no, it is not in my power." Now leave all these with God, and meddle not with them, but put them over to the Lord, and meddle with thine own duty, and thine own work; and let God alone with his. And say thou unto the Lord, " in truth, Lord, it is not in my power, it is not in my parts or work, either to compass that wisdom, that is able to direct myself, or to have any power to do all that is commanded, much less to give good success. Lord, I will not meddle with that, but leave it with thy majesty : if thou in thy power canst not, nor in thy faithfulness and goodness carest not for thy poor helpless creature, then I am content: and if thou wilt not be faithful, then I am content to be miserable."

And so also thou mayest suppose a man that hath promised to undertake some business for a friend, and in the end it proves somewhat troublesome, and therefore he wishes his friend to take it again into his own hands ; for it is very troublesome. But a man will leave it to him, and say, he hath engaged himself to do it, and he will not look after it ; I will not meddle with it any more. So whatever it is that is in God's royal prerogative, leave it with God, and do not meddle with it. Let God now look to it ; leave it to his faithfulness and power to accomplish it. So did Abraham, Rom. 4 : 16—20. *Who against hope* [or, above] *hope, believed in* [or, under] *hope, that he should become the father of many nations.* Sarah's womb was barren, and his body dead, and yet he must have a son : and therefore he sets God's power at work, and saith, verse 21, " Lord, this body is dead, and Sarah is barren : there is no help here : but thou art able, and thou hast engaged thyself to do it." You see he sets God's power to work, and puts over all the weight and burthen of the care upon the Lord. And therefore says Mordecai, Esther 4 : 14. *If thou altogether holdest thy peace at this time, enlargement and deliverance shall come from some other place.* He was resolved that God had deliverance for his church, and would not deny his truth. Salvation will come, saith the text. He knows not the place or the means : but he knows salvation will come. So set thou God's power and faithfulness to work, and not thy own care : commit it to the Lord, and cast thy care upon him, so far as concerns the burthen of it.

2. By faith go to the promise again for help

and power to wait on God in that way, and to
look towards God in the use of those means, he
hath appointed for the attaining of that good
which his power will work for thee. God will
certainly work it : and so thou must meet God in
the course of his providence, in the improvement
of the means he hath appointed for thy good.
Observe thou his providence, and do thou what
God requires. For otherwise we live not by
faith, but tempt God, and throw away the promise and all, and deprive ourselves of that good
which God would bestow ; we not walking in
that way which he hath appointed. Luke 24 :
49, when our Saviour was to go to heaven, he
said, *behold, I send the promise of my Father
amongst you : but tarry you in the city of Jerusalem, until you be endued with power from above.*
Christ would endue them with the Spirit ; but
they must tarry at Jerusalem and wait for it. So
I say, wouldst thou have grace and the Spirit
from above, and the wealth of the world ? Then
walk in that way God hath appointed : stay at
Jerusalem, and be in the way, and meet God in
his providence ; and then thou shalt receive from
his power and faithfulness what thou needest.
Thou wouldst have God bless thee in thine
estate, and yet thou wouldst be idle and careless :
but this will not do the deed : God would give
thee a blessing, but thou art not there to take it.

This is the excellency of the promises of God ; as they require conditions before they bestow mercies, so they make us able to be partakers of the conditions, and give the conditions : as for example, Ezek. 36, the Lord in the former part of the chapter promiseth to give them many things ; but how ? It must be by prayer, and humbling themselves before him. He will give thee a family blessing, by prayer in it ; and a blessing in private, by prayer in private ; and strength against sin, and power against corruption. But I will be sought unto for all these, saith the Lord : and the text saith, Prov. 20 : 7. *Blessed is the man that walketh in his integrity, and his children after him.* Therefore walk thou in the integrity of thine heart ; that is the condition of a Christian in general ; or as a husband, or as a wife, or as a servant, in the particular. This the promise requires. But mark this now : the same promise that requireth the conditions, will help us to perform the conditions. And the same Lord that saith, *I will be entreated and sought to for these ;* the same Lord saith, Psalm 10 : 17. *He prepareth their hearts to pray.* Go thou therefore to God to help thee to pray, that he may bestow his blessing upon thee, which he hath promised, Ezek. 26 : 27, he will first give them a new heart, then teach them to walk in his ways. So if thou wilt walk in his ways, thou shalt have his bles-

sings.   Therefore go thou by the power of faith,
to the promises of God, for strength and grace,
and in that thou must use the means appointed;
and then expect a blessing from it in the course
of his providence.   Now is God's power and
faithfulness set a-work.

3. We must set it down, and conclude it, that
God will do it ; so shall we receive in the ways
of his providence whatsoever he hath promised to
give.   That is the work of faith, and that is to
draw sap and virtue from the promise, John 3 : 33.
*He that hath received his testimony, hath set to
his seal that God is true.*   There, by sealing, is
meant sealing to the promise.   This is the nature
of sealing ; when a man hath drawn the articles
of agreement, and when they have been sealed,
the whole matter is done.   So faith must make
the promise authentical, and put a seal to it that
it is true ; and saith, " it is done in heaven, and I
am fully resolved, and settledly persuaded thereof,
that I shall have whatever I have believed ; and
thou, Lord, hast promised, and I have used the
means in the ways of thy providence."   Famous
is that of Abraham, Gen. 22: 5.   The Lord hath
bidden him sacrifice his son, and yet had said before he should live.   And therefore when he
came to the place, he said to his servants, *abide
you here with the asses ; for I and the lad will go
yonder, and sacrifice, and return again to you.*

He thought to sacrifice him, and yet by faith he believed that he should bring Isaac again. So I would have a poor saint of God believe and conclude. When thou findest thy comfort like Isaac's in the ashes, and thy estate helpless and hopeless; yet even then set God's power a-work, and wait upon him in the use of the means he hath appointed, and there conclude it, and that He will bring patience, power, and deliverance, and so in every kind, according to all necessities. Yet remember this, expect no more from the promise, than God will give in the promise: but say, " my sins shall be mastered one day, and these temptations shall one day be overthrown, that have so long annoyed the soul of thy servant. I have begged succour against these corruptions within, and these temptations without, and yet it is not; but I know it is done in heaven; it wants nothing but the taking out. Thou wilt bestow upon thy servant what thou seest fit." 1 Sam. 1: 18. Hannah wept sore, and prayed to the Lord, and went away, and was no more sorrowful: and she said, " Lord, I believe that I shall either have a child, or that which is as good, or better;" now the business was done. But suppose the Lord delays, and does not suddenly accomplish what he intends, and thou hast used means to receive; he gives not, grants not, sends not succour according to

thy desire, and the tenor of the covenant, as thou
conceivest.

4. Then faith is to take up its stand, and stay
till it come : as thou resolvest, so it will be. Stay
till it be, and stay it out.   Here is much work to
do.   We prevent God's kindness, when we go
away before he be willing to bestow a kindness
on us.   But faith will not do so.   He that be-
lieves, does not make haste.   He makes haste to
obey, but he stays, and resolves that it will be.
Hab. 2 : 3.   *The vision is for an appointed time;
but at the end it shall speak, and not lie ; therefore wait for it, because it will surely come.*
Thou art pestered with thy sins, and hast laboured by faith to subdue them; and thy estate is
low, and thou hast laboured by faith for deliverance : and yet it comes not.   Therefore stay till
God sees fit, and it will come.   Psalm 123 : 2.
*As the eyes of servants look to the hands of their
masters, and as the eyes of a maiden to the hand
of her mistress ; so our eyes wait upon the Lord
our God, until he have mercy upon us.*   It is not,
till I will, or till I see fit, or according to my
mind; but until the Lord have mercy.   We suddenly slide away from the covenant which the
Lord makes with us; because we have it not
when we will, therefore we go away.   1 Samuel
13 : 13.   When Samuel tarried long, and the

people began to murmur, Saul went and offered
a burnt-offering to the Lord : and therefore Samuel said unto him, *thou hast done foolishly, thou
hast not kept the commandment of the Lord thy
God, which he commanded thee; for now would
the Lord have established thy kingdom upon Israel
forever.* If Saul had stayed the Lord's time, He
would have established his kingdom upon Israel
forever. But he prevented the Lord's kindness,
and offered sacrifice unseasonably and sinfully.
So it is many times with a proud, pettish, rash
and distempered heart : if we have not what we
would, and when we would, then we are all
amort, *i. e.* quite dead-hearted, and murmur, and
say, why should we wait any longer ? Thou hast
done foolishly ; hast thou prayed and looked to
the promise thus long, and wilt thou now give
over ? The Lord would have comforted thee,
hadst thou gone on. But the Lord hath with-
drawn himself from thee, because thou hast with-
drawn thy heart from the promise. When the
carriage is heavy, and the way dead, there are
many sore pulls, and oft the waggon is at a stand ;
and if a man should then go away and give over,
all his work were lost. Therefore stay thou till
the Lord show mercy. Thus long thou hast
called and sought, and looked up to the promise,
and waited upon the Lord, and attended upon the
freeness of his grace. Once more haply would

have done it : thy heart was almost humbled, thy sin was almost conquered. Oh thou silly soul, why didst not thou hold it out? It would have come at the last ; my life for thine. Now take heed of this ; if the time seems tedious, and thy heart begins to sink, and thy spirit is weary ; take heed of flying off, take heed of shifting for thy own comfort, and looking to base ends and aims. No, hold thy mind to, and keep thy eye of faith upon the promise, and stay it out till God see the time fit. And know, it is the best time, when it is God's time. In the 27th of the Acts, verse 31, Paul says, *except these abide in the ship, ye cannot be saved.* Every man was skipping overboard to save himself, but Paul stayed them. A man would have thought otherwise; but the apostle knew it was not so ; for the Lord had revealed it to him. So I say, be thy temptations ever so strong, and thy sins ever so many, and thou beginnest to complain, and sayest, " I have cried, Lord, and sought earnestly, and yet my condition is worse, and my soul more sinful, and I am less able to help myself, there is no more succour to be expected." Now take heed of going out of the ship, and from the use of means. Keep in the ship ; for in it you shall be safe. Keep in the promise, and still your hearts there. You shall have a happy arrival at heaven, though it be upon a little broken board.   It is no matter, stay God's time.

5. Lay hold on God in Christ, and wrestle with him, and never let him go.   For yet haply the Lord seems not only to delay his poor servants, and to withhold his favour ; but he seems to frown and say, he will not hear.   And he seems to be angry with the prayer of his servants, and with their importunity ; and as if he would not succour and supply : thus he dealt with Jacob, Gen. 32 : 26.   There the Lord says, let me go ; I care not what becomes of thee, let me go : but Jacob lays hold upon him, and would not let him go.   So the last work of faith is this, in a holy humility labour to contend with God, and by a strong hand overcome the Lord ; for the Lord loves to be overcome thus.   Be not saucy* with the Lord.   But in the sense of thine own baseness, as it were, lay hold upon the Lord Jesus, and strive with him ; leave not till thou hast those comforts he hath promised, and thou hast begged. This is the glory and the victory of the triumph of faith, that gives thee the day ; and the Lord, as it were, lays down the weapons, and yields himself as conquered.   As it was with Jacob, when God saw he could not prevail, he said, verse 28.   *Thy name shall no more be called*

* Irreverent.   Ed.

Jacob, *but Israel*, *because thou hast prevailed
with God*. God is ready to give what he hath
promised; but he will have us try the mastery
with him. God overcomes himself, and we by
faith in God, overcome or prevail with God : as
James 2: 13. *Mercy triumphs over justice.*
"Lord," saith my soul " why should not I have
that mercy, supply and succour ?" Saith justice,
"thou art a sinful wretch, and thou hast wronged
me." Saith anger, "thou hast deserved to be
plagued ; and therefore thou shalt feel the smart
of my displeasure." Now faith lays hold upon
the riches of the freeness of God's mercy in Christ ;
and in him justice is satisfied, and anger appeased
for all. And now mercy is purchased for all, and
mercy triumpheth over justice ; and faith takes
hold upon and overcomes God himself, as I may
say, with a holy, humble baseness of heart. You
know what the Lord did to the woman of Canaan,
Matthew 15 : 28, when she had striven with him
a great while, and would take no denial ; at last
he saith, *O woman, great is thy faith, be it unto
thee even as thou wilt.* "Take what thou wilt ;
if thou wilt have life for thy child, and peace for
thine own conscience, and joy in the Holy Ghost,
take it ; for it is all thine." He, as it were, turns
her loose to all his treasury. If she had gone
away at the first or second denial, she had found
no help ; but because she held out, she had all

her heart's desire. God would have us wrestle
with his majesty, that he may be overcome in
mercy and goodness.

I might have here taken some of the most desperate cases that could be, that you might have
seen what faith would have done in the midst of
the want of all means, and in the greatest extremity that could have befallen a poor sinner;
but I pass over that at this time.

Now therefore consider what hath been said:
lay these things up, and have them ever before
you, and practise them: and by often writing,
learn to write: and by often living, learn to live.
Many people live poorly, and make a poor shift
to go to heaven. I would not have a Christian
live so, but be master of his art. Know and see
your way, and use the means. Labour to get
good thereby; that you may have the sap and
sweet of the promises, and so go singing and re-
joicing and triumphing up to heaven.

The Conclusion

Now that which I conclude withal is this: you see how far the Lord hath brought us; how the soul hath been prepared, and cut off from sin and itself, if fitted for the Lord Jesus, by contrition and humiliation; and that the soul comes to see that there is no hope in the creatures, nor any succour in heaven, but in the Lord Jesus Christ. And so at last the sinner comes, and lies at the foot of the Lord Jesus, and knows that either he must be another man, or a damned man. Now when he sees that prayer and all other means will not profit, and the power of the means yet prevails not, and the power of his corruptions is not yet mastered; then he looks up to Christ, and is contented that he should do what he will with him. Now when the Lord Jesus sees him lie wearied thus with his corruptions, then the Lord gives special notice to his soul that it is his purpose to do him good, and that there is mercy for that broken heart of his. With that hope is stirred; and faith cries out, " is it possible? Is it credible? Shall this wretchedness of mine be pardoned? Oh, my desire is kindled within me, and I long for that day: O that I might once see the funeral of all my sins!" Mark now how love and joy are cheered to entertain this mercy ; and oh how is the soul bound and engaged to God, that offers free and undeserved grace to a stubborn and rebellious sinner ! At last the will saith amen to the promise ; and further saith, O that mercy I will have ! And thus the soul is come home to God by vocation. Now the prodigal is come home to his father ; and the father's heart leaps within his breast, when he sees him lie at the door. And as the Father rejoiceth, so the angels in heaven rejoice ; and all the faithful shall rejoice, and say, " oh my husband, oh my father, oh my child, and oh my wife, that was a sinful woman, is come home again to her first and best husband." You that have found it thus in yourselves, be comforted. You that know it in others, rejoice.

To sum up all briefly, we see,

First ; when we have plucked away all carnal props, then there is way made for the promise to come in to us.

Secondly ; and when our hearts are possessed thoroughly of the sufficiency of God's promise and grace, then the promise that draws near, begins its work.

Thirdly ; that when we expect all from the promise, even power to come to it, then it lays fast hold upon us.

Fourthly ; that when we are content to yield

to the just conditions of the promise, then the promise carries us, and all in us.

Thus we have seen the hinderances removed, and the means propounded. And hence we see, that faith is to be laboured for above all graces. And now that we may be moved and persuaded importunately to seek after this blessed grace of God, let us further consider thus much, namely, that if we once get this grace, we get all other graces with it ; which is a ground of much comfort, and cannot but keep us doing. For will it not much encourage a man, when in the doing of one work he knows he shall do another, nay, all his work with one labour ! But so it is in the work of faith. Oh then how should it encourage us to labour for faith, seeing that by getting it, we have all ? Men that are wise to provide for themselves, and to lay out their monies in some purchase for the best ; when they see a ground well wooded and watered, but especially to have some rich mines in it, all their minds will be upon such a place, because, having it, they have all with it. So it should be here, in our desires ; and as there, so here ; get this grace, and get all. Strengthen here, and all is strong : but want here, and want every where. Having this grace of faith, you need not seek for wisdom ; for faith will make you wise to salvation. And you need not labour for patience ; for he that is faithful, will be patient; and so for other graces. He that hath the grace of faith, hath them all; hath holiness, hath cleanness, hath love, hath a pure mind, and good conscience; and what hath he not? The saints of God endeavour with much pains to get grace, and to subdue corruption. But because they take not the right way to it, they seek and do not find.

Many a poor soul mourns and cries to heaven for mercy, and prays against a stubborn hard heart, and is weary of his life, because this vile heart remains yet in him; and yet haply gets little or no redress. The reason is, and the main wound lies here; he goes the wrong way to work; for, he that would have grace must (first of all) get faith. Faith will bring all the rest. Buy the field and the pearl is thine; it goes with the purchase. Thou must not think with thine own struggling to get the mastery of a proud heart; for that will not do. But let thy faith go first to Christ, and try what that can do. There are many graces necessary in this work; as meekness, patience, humility, and wisdom: now faith will fetch all these, and possess the soul of them. Brethren, therefore if you set any price upon these graces, buy the field, labour for faith; get that, and you get all. The apostle saith, 2 Cor. 3 : 18. *We all with open face, beholding as in a glass, the glory of the Lord, are changed into the*

same image, from glory to glory. The Lord
Christ is the glass, and the glorious grace of God
in Christ, is that glory of the Lord. Therefore
first behold this grace in Christ by faith (and thou
must do so before thou canst receive grace.)
First, see humility in Christ, and then draw it
thence. First, see strength and courage in him,
whereby to enable thy weak heart, and strength
will come ; there fetch it, and there have it.
Would you then have a meek, gracious, and humble heart ? I dare say for some of you, that you
had rather have it than any thing under heaven,
and would think it the best bargain that ever you
made ; which is the cause why you say, " O that
I could once see that day, that this proud heart
of mine might be humbled : oh if I could see the
last blood of my sins, I should then think myself
happy, none more, and desire to live no longer."
But is this thy desire, poor soul ? Then get
faith, and so buy the whole, for they all go together : nor think to have them upon any price,
not having faith : I mean patience, and meekness,
and the humble heart. But buy faith, the field,
and you have the pearl. Further, would you
have the glory of God in your eye, and be more
heavenly-minded ? Then look to it, and get it by
the eye of faith. Look up to it in the face of
Jesus Christ, and then you shall see it ; and then
hold you there. For there, and there only, this

vision of the glory of God is to be seen, to your everlasting peace and endless comfort. When men use to make a purchase, they speak of all the commodities of it ; as, that there is so much wood, worth so much ; and so much stock, worth so much ; and then they offer for the whole, answerable to these severals. So here ; there is item for an heavenly mind, and that is worth thousands ; and, item for an humble heart, and that is worth millions. And so for the rest. And are those graces so much worth ? What is faith worth then ? Hence we may conclude and say, O precious faith ! precious indeed, that is able, through the Spirit of Christ, to bring so many, nay, all graces with it ; as one degree of grace after another, grace here, and happiness for ever hereafter. If we have but the hearts of men (I do not say of Christians) methinks this that is spoken of faith, should provoke us to labour always, above all things, for this blessed grace of God, the grace of faith.

First Meeting House in Connecticut.

The above is believed to be a correct representation of the first house ever erected in Connecticut for Christian worship, built in 1635. Some of the lumber of the first house is still in existence, a portion of it being used in the construction of the Centre Congregational Church.

Rev. Thomas Hooker's House.

The above is a front view of the house of Rev. Thomas Hooker, first minister of the gospel in Connecticut. The projection in front (A) was called the porch, and was used as his study. The building stood on the north side of School street, and the drawing was taken immediately before it was taken down